Telling Stories to Children

A National Storytelling Guide

Editor
Betty Lehrman

Designer
Karen Wollscheid

Illustration
Brandt Studios

Produced under the direction of
Glenn Morrow, NSN Board Liaison and
Chair, Communications Committee
and
the National Storytelling Press Committee
Joan Kimball, Chair
Sharon Creeden
Jill Johnson
Judy Sima

National Storytelling Press
a division of
National Storytelling Network

ISBN: 1-879991-34-9

Published by
National Storytelling Press

Distributed by
National Storytelling Network
132 Boone Street
Jonesborough TN 37659
Toll Free: 1-800-525-4514
Direct: 423-913-8201
E-mail: nsn@storynet.org
Website: www.storynet.org

The National Storytelling Network (NSN)
is a member organization which supports
storytellers and storytelling throughout
the US through grants and services. NSN
sponsors the National Storytelling Conference
each July and the annual "Tellabration," which brings
storytelling to hundreds of locations every November.
NSN publishes *Storytelling Magazine*, the *NSN Source Book*,
guides to storytelling, and story collections on books and
recorded media. Members can join Special Interest Groups
on storytelling in schools, higher education, organizations
and business, healing arts, and planning for festivals and
events. The Network is co-owner of the National Storytelling
Festival, held each October in Jonesborough, Tennessee.

Welcome!

The phrases "once upon a time" and "happily ever after" were given to the world between 1812 and 1815 by linguists Jacob and Wilhelm Grimm. They are magical phrases filled with awesome possibilities. Stories can make impressions that last a lifetime. They can be entertaining, informative, and educational. Stories promote literacy, fluency, empathy, and the joy of "once upon a time."

The National Storytelling Network is pleased to offer this publication, the second in a series of storytelling guides. *Telling Stories to Children* follows the first guide, *A Beginner's Guide to Storytelling,* and covers a wide variety of topics and techniques concerning telling stories to children in pre-school through grade eight. This resource is a valuable tool for parents, teachers, librarians, amateur and professional storytellers – in fact, anyone wishing to relate stories to children.

The mission of the National Storytelling Network is to bring together and nurture individuals who use the power of storytelling in all its forms. **Telling Stories to Children** comprises articles written by practicing storytellers around the country. Each article is welcoming. We invite you to experience the magic.

Diane Williams, Chair
National Storytelling Network Board of Directors

Acknowledgments

Our collaboration on this, the second storytelling guide for NSN, has given us many enjoyable moments. We have benefited from the planning and insight of NSN Press Committee members Jill Johnson, Sharon Creeden, and Judy Sima; the guidance of our board liaison, Glenn Morrow; and the experience of NSN Executive Director Karen Dietz. Our hats are off to our extremely capable (and amazingly quick!) graphic designer, Karen Wollscheid (storybiz@earthlink.net), who planned the first NSN guide, *A Beginner's Guide to Storytelling*, and has again turned the authors' words into a visually inviting publication. Our greatest thanks go to the writers who generously volunteered their expertise, creating a rich collection of inspired approaches and nuts-and-bolts suggestions for storytelling.

Betty Lehrman, Editor
Joan Kimball, Press Committee Chair

Contents

Foreword

When I was a librarian, I generally read stories aloud. One day, however, I chose to *tell* "Jack and the Beanstalk." Working up to the "Fee, fi, foe," part in the story, I found I was closer than ever to the children. An electric current crackled between us. Books are great, but telling a story without the book is a unique experience that grips teller and listener; it is a primal human act.

Some of our folktales were probably told by the first humans in Africa fifty thousand years ago. Today we keep the ancient tales alive and create our own. We are the living breath of a story's existence that will be alive a thousand – even fifty thousand – years from now.

Whether you tell folktales, personal stories, historical tales, or simple anecdotes, this guide is designed to inform, liberate, and inspire you in your telling to children. A dad driving kids to a game, a teacher introducing a math formula, a performer facing fifty families in a library, a grandmother recalling her youth, a nurse imparting courage: all these connect with their listeners through the electricity of storytelling. Read this book cover to cover, or pick and choose your chapters. The authors are long-time storytellers who share their secrets with beginners and experienced tellers alike.

Joan Kimball, Chair
National Storytelling Network
Press Committee

Playful Storytelling with the Young Child

by Annette Harrison

Ihave been telling stories for twenty-six years and am still amazed by the ability of storytelling to keep young listeners entranced. The eye contact, the grand gestures, the expressive face and body, the inflection of the voice all combine to create a joyous storytelling experience. As soon as the story begins, listeners' eyes grow big as saucers and they are transported into the world of story.

In 1976 I took a workshop with storyteller Lynn Rubright and was so inspired by it that with a repertoire of just three tales I went knocking on pre-school doors. I was surprised: even though the children already knew these stories, they were immediately attentive. I had tapped into something primal, something universal, with a strong connection between me, the story, and the children. At one telling a child grabbed onto my skirt, looked up at me and asked, "Will you be my Mommy?" Needless to say, I was hooked!

Youngest Listeners

It is never too early to share stories with babies one-to-one, but at a center or pre-school my youngest audience is slightly under two years old. When telling to two-year-olds, start with familiar stories. I always begin with "The Three Bears." They watch me as I line up three chairs. Then we count them together "1-2-3!" "Look, I have three chairs, do you know what I am going to tell?" Then I tell the story in a playful, interactive way. I use counting, silly noises, and funny voices as ways of keeping their attention, always checking to see if they are with me.

For two- to three-year-olds, individual stories should be short, no longer than eight minutes. And programs should be no more than thirty minutes. Four- to five-year-olds can enjoy more sophisticated stories and slightly longer programs. But even with six-year-olds who listen attentively to a variety of folktales and fairy tales, six to eight minute stories work the best.

Be Yourself

This sounds simple, but it is so important. Unless you are speaking in character, remember to use your natural speaking voice and speak directly to the audience. Young children need to hear and trust you, the storyteller, first. As you experiment with delivery, voice, and gestures, stay in your comfort zone. This will expand as you tell stories more often. You will be amazed as you grow from that comfortable place and develop your own style.

Energy, Enthusiasm, and Playfulness

Follow the EEP of storytelling: Energy, Enthusiasm, and Playfulness. My wise mentor, Lynn Rubright, had a drama teacher who said, "It's all in the energy." I agree. Gather your positive energy and focus it on your storytelling: be bigger than life!

Let the children know that *this* is the place you want to be and *they* are the audience you want to be with. Your enthusiasm will shine through. I am constantly told that the children are swept up in my enthusiastic telling.

I can't emphasize enough how important it is to be playful. Be open to improvisation when you tell to young children; do not memorize your story. React to what they say and do as you share with them. Remember, they understand play, they learn through play; so *play* with them in the storytelling process.

Connect with Your Audience

When you tell to young children, *connect* with them first.

Because you are a stranger in their midst, they need to know that you are friendly and want to share with them. When the children are coming into the performance or you are entering their space, greet them with direct eye contact, a smile, and a wave. I do this even with large audiences, although in a childcare center or pre-school I try to tell in the individual rooms. It is a lot easier to connect when children are in small groups.

Focus the children's attention by singing a song with them, playing a musical instrument, or mentioning something they can all relate to, such as the weather, the season, or an upcoming holiday. I often ask a question that leads into a story, such as, "Did you ever wonder where the snow comes from? Here's a story that answers that question."

Active Involvement

To keep pre-schoolers happy and attentive, they must be actively involved.

- Teach them rhythms or songs that are repeated throughout the story. Do this before the story is told or during the telling with the words "repeat after me."
- Lead them in hand or body movements for walking, hopping, slithering, sliding, galloping, or dancing. Vary the pace and exaggerate the movements. Funny faces are encouraged! Make sure you tell them whether you want them to stay in their places or move around the room.
- Use funny sounds such as snores, thunder claps, hisses, chuckles, snorts, or moos. Warn the youngest ones that a loud noise is coming.
- Give them a magic word to listen for, such as 'No!' When they hear the word, they can clap, touch their noses, shake their heads, or even jump up and twirl around.
- Let the children fill in the blanks for you. You might say, "Baby Bear looked at his bed and said, ' _____.'"
- Ask direct questions. For example, "Would you like to make snow with the snow bears?" Be prepared to field their answers!

Be clear about when and how to end the participation and balance it with quiet listening so that the story line is not lost.

Appropriate Stories

When picking a story, choose one that you love and that is age appropriate. Look for:

- a simple plot that is easy to follow, with each incident related to the plot
- quick action, surprises, and humor
- a small number of well-defined characters
- vivid word pictures
- events children can relate to
- repetition and parts for interaction
- an ending that resolves the conflict and leaves the children feeling satisfied

Note: Don't neglect the familiar fairy tales. It is the birthright of all children to know these literary basics.

Additional Considerations

- Find out classroom themes and choose stories accordingly.
- Know your story well. Learn the plot and flesh out the characters so that you can play in the story. Practice!
- Jazz up your telling with music, puppets, or props. My rule of thumb: whatever works!
- Always leave on a positive note. Even with negative experiences, find something kind to say before you go.

Welcome to the magic circle of storytelling and to our greatest resource, young children. Jump into the experience with both feet and have fun!

*Annette Harrison is a performer, author, and educator. She has published **Easy-to-Tell Stories** (National Storytelling Press, 1992 – winner, Benjamin Franklin Education Award) and, with Jerilynn Changar, PhD, **Storytelling Activities Kit** (Prentice Hall, 1992). Her newest venture is **Stories to the Rescue** with Ruthilde Kronberg. NetHarBar@aol.com*

Reading Readiness and Literacy

by Carole Tallant

One challenge facing parents and teachers today is how to instill a love of reading in children in an era of video games, television, and computers. Jim Trelease, author of *The Read Aloud Handbook*[1], shows that we can help children become lifelong readers through spoken language. He offers eye-opening statistics that suggest a correlation between illiteracy and imprisonment. His determination is that we need to convince children that carrying books is infinitely more rewarding than carrying guns.

How do we, as parents, teachers, concerned citizens, and *storytellers* help children develop a desire to read? I don't pretend to have the definitive answer, but in my twenty-four years of teaching storytelling and the performance of literature, I have found one sure-fire way to kindle a child's desire to "make friends" with books – storytelling!

Hearing stories enhances a child's ability to speak, write, and read. In the May/June 2003 *Storytelling Magazine*, Jeannine Pasini Beekman[2] tells us that storytelling not only improves listening skills and exposes children to enriched language, but it also helps them associate written symbols with the words they are hearing. Skillful storytelling teaches literary sequencing and encourages children to visualize images embodied in the story. Scholar Jack Zipes, in *Creative Storytelling*[3], states that there are certain "grammatical rules" of the imagination that children must learn before they can successfully process and create stories. It is in hearing the stories performed that children absorb insights into story structure.

Teachers report that when children hear traditional stories such as "Jack and the Varmints," they subliminally recognize key structural components of the story (e.g., beginning, middle, and end), as well as crisis and climax moments. Although they may lack labels for such elements, children begin to incorporate them into their own stories and are better able to recognize them in stories they read. In addition, hearing stories has been shown to enhance children's ability to speak, write, and read with greater acuity and precision.

Each semester I teach college students in a service-learning course called "Storytelling in the Community." Students tell stories in local elementary schools once a week for eleven weeks. We strive to excite children about reading, build vocabulary and visual images, and diminish any apprehensions about the reading process.

By exciting children about the performed stories, we interest them in the books they've "heard." I encourage the student storytellers to use enthusiasm and effective storytelling skills to connect with their listeners. I ask students who can sing, dance, play musical instruments, or juggle to consider enhancing their telling with those talents. One student used his magician's skills to retell "Jack and the Beanstalk" as "Magic Jack and the Beanstalk," creating unexpected illusions to illustrate the fairytale. Teachers report that the children often request library visits so they can "check out the books the storyteller told."

The everyday language used in conversation is appropriate for casual, informal interactions, but when language is placed within a performance frame, crafting enriches it. This doesn't mean that storytellers should sound as if they have swallowed a dictionary, but that they should devote significant time to creating vivid mental pictures. Compare the two sentences: "The coins fell out of her mouth," as opposed to, "The coins cascaded from her ruby lips." Clearly, the second sentence brings the image more vividly to life. I use storyteller Heather Forest's book, *Wonder Tales from Around the World*[4], to demonstrate the kind of language I want students to use. For instance, in "The Magic Brocade," a weaver creates silk brocades that are so lifelike, the woven birds almost "quivered." People who see the brocades "gasp at their beauty and grasp for their purses." These carefully selected words create a verbal feast for our ears.

Sometimes my students question the use of sophisticated language with younger children. Although they have a limited speaking vocabulary, children's comprehension of what they hear far outstrips their verbal abilities. Trelease offers the example that when the original "Cosby" show aired, whole families would watch it together. "Cosby" generally used a fourth grade vocabulary. Still, kindergartners could enjoy the weekly antics because their understanding of language went far beyond their ability to use it.

Another goal of my course is to diminish apprehension about the reading process. Many of the schools in which we perform have significant at-risk populations. These children, often from homes where neglect and lack of support are the defining features, are well aware of their own difficulties in mastering reading and writing. In my work with such children, I witness some who joyfully engage in reading aloud without fear or trepidation, as well as children who struggle with each word and sound, clearly agonizing over their embarrassment about reading in front of others.

Children can embrace the enjoyment of reading by experiencing how their imaginations help them respond to printed words. In storytelling, words and pictures can leap off the pages of a book. Hearing and seeing literature creatively performed opens children's eyes to the beauty and power of language. When they see that words aren't merely black and white symbols, but avenues to splendid images, some of their anxiety about reading is alleviated.

Lewis Carroll writes that stories are "gifts" we share with children. One of the best ways to unwrap those gifts is through audience participation. Having children repeat chants, sing songs, mimic gestures and actions, answer questions, or even become a character in a story increases their involvement in the stories.

The classic picture book, *Crictor*[5], contains a participatory story wonderful for stimulating beginning reading. Madame Bodot receives Crictor the boa constrictor from her son. After becoming fast friends with the snake, Madame Bodot brings it to the elementary school where she teaches. Crictor becomes a visual aid to Mme. Bodot in illustrating letters and numbers. As the story progresses, I manipulate my five-foot long stuffed snake into letters and numbers such as *O, P, M*, and *2*. Children eagerly "guess" what Crictor is demonstrating, becoming excited to "read" within the story.

We as storytellers have the ability to connect with children in face-to-face communication that brings them into the compelling world of literature. Through stories, children may learn the tools to help them love reading, preparing them for a life-long relationship with books. As Beekman reminds us, "working with children is akin to a sacred calling. They deserve the very best we can ever offer to any audience." I believe that our best is no less than storytelling.

Notes

1. Jim Trelease, *The Read-Aloud Handbook*. 5th edition. NY: Penguin Books, 2001.
2. Jeannine Pasini Beekman, "Telling and Crafting Stories for Young Listeners." *Storytelling Magazine* (National Storytelling Network) Vol. 15, No. 3 (2003): 27-35.
3. Jack Zipes, *Creative Storytelling*. NY: Routledge, 1995.
4. Heather Forest, *Wonder Tales From Around the World*. Little Rock, AR: August House, 1995.
5. Tomi Ungerer, *Crictor*. NY: HarperCollins, 1986, c1958.

Carole Tallant *is a professor of Communication Studies at the University of North Carolina at Wilmington where she specializes in courses about performance of children's literature and storytelling. She was named the 2004 Carnegie Foundation for the Advancement of Teaching North Carolina Professor of the Year. tallantc@uncw.edu*

Family Story Land: History and Identity

by Gail N. Herman

"**D**ad, who's Uncle Dave?" "Mom, who's that lady in the picture?" "What did Nana mean about her 'orphanage'?" Our daughter Leta wanted to know more about our family, and so we began our journey into family story land. Whether relating silly stories, laughing at mistakes, or explaining family traits, telling stories together is a great way to create a feeling of belonging and a sense of identity.

Family storytelling encourages self-confidence in a child. To begin, tell stories about the bright, smart things he did when he was small. Even failed attempts at excellence are worthy of retelling. For example, you might tell about the time your toddler was so "athletic" she decided to throw "the *biiiiig* football." Describe how she approached it, caressed it, looked under it, tried to pick it up, and how it was almost as big as she was! Describe the proud look on her face when the ball rolled out of her arms. Even though this is only an anecdote, it might someday become part of a larger story about her love of sports.

Tell about events that happened to you, yourself, when you were younger. Tell about the time you got into trouble (a before-I-knew-better story) or a time you were really, really scared (a before-I-was-old-enough-to-be-brave story). One way to end these stories is to tell about what you learned from the event. Another is to give them a humorous slant. These stories teach our children that making a mistake or being scared is human; after all, even we, their parents, did this. And they see that we can look at our own mistakes with humor.

Tell stories about when your child was younger and did something silly. These stories allow children to objectify situations so that they can laugh at themselves, examine their actions, and most importantly, know that they would never make *that* mistake again. When told lovingly and with the attitude, "now you are bigger and know better," these stories can be healthy and fun. Children love to retell them, as well.

Photos can inspire stories. A mother I know discovered a picture of her son standing in the sink with bubbles up to his elbows. She narrated how "Bubbles Goba" (the family name was Goba) had sneaked over and climbed up onto the counter to "wash" the dishes. Everyone had just laughed and laughed at his seriousness as he scrubbed. She ended the story by saying how his dedicated dishwashing was a good example of her family's clean gene! Out of the many, many incidents in the boy's life, this particular one was recalled and retold, perhaps because it exemplified a trait of which the older generations were proud. The story addressed two tale types: it was a "before-I-knew-better story" and it explained a family attribute.

My mother-in-law, Nana, wrote a memoir about her family history, her immigration, and her experience in an orphanage. My daughter Leta loved to hear Nana's tales told and later she loved to read them herself. In the stories Leta found many positive traits, including courage, creativity, resiliency, forgiveness, and dignity.

For ten years Nana and her brother lived in foster homes and in an orphanage. During this time, Nana encountered some very caring adults as well as adults and older children who were less than kind. In one story, she pretended to be a Pollyanna wearing rose-colored glasses in order to annoy her adversaries. She "wore" the glasses when her "big sisters" gave her unjust tasks. "Actually, I am happy to clean the bathroom instead of going to the silent movies; I need a night home to write my letters, anyway!" she said.

Still another story reveals her creative solutions. No one was allowed to eat in school unless there was enough for everyone. Nana wanted apples to eat so she tucked away enough for everyone in her clothes. Was that teacher surprised when forty-plus apples tumbled out from the girl's bloomers!

After discovering my mother-in-law's journal I was inspired to begin one myself. I bought a big, blank book and any time I went to my various relatives' homes for holidays, I wrote down the stories and anecdotes as I heard them told. I would find a blank page and write the date and the narrator's name. Then I would start writing, not worrying about mechanics or style, just focusing on the core of the story. I didn't write every word, just the essentials. Eventually, family members began to sidle up to me to share stories. The book went to weddings, baptisms, and Bar Mitzvahs. If I forgot the book, I'd write on paper napkins!

I plan to pass the book along to my daughter, and perhaps she will pass it along to her son, who is beginning to love stories. I hope my stories are as interesting as Nana's, and will inspire more recording of and listening to family stories in the future.

When we tell stories about our relatives, ancestors, and our children, we send a clear message to the younger generation: you are part of a real life story, an epic tale of joys, trials, tribulations, and triumphs. Our ancestors' stories are the building blocks, the DNA, of personal identity. Family storytelling links generations together, connecting each child's life to the lives lived before and after. The stories are gifts given to children and passed from them to the next generation.

Dr. Gail N. Herman performs her family stories for students in grades K-8 and conducts storytelling and writing residencies. Her students learn that they must tell their stories in order to discover what they need to write and rewrite. gnherman@gcnetmail.net

Bedtime Stories

by Naomi Leithold

A cup of hot tea. A book or an old movie. And a big, warm blanket. That's all you can think about at the end of a long day, but that doesn't fit into your child's agenda. Even though her day has been as exhausting as yours, she still wants to do an art project, build a castle, bake a cake, and run a few laps around your basement. It is clear that putting this bundle of energy into bed, saying good-night, and turning off the lights will have disastrous results. Wind-down time is definitely required.

A bedtime routine that includes storytelling can fill this need. After pajamas are on and teeth are brushed, treat your child to an oral story instead of her usual book. Telling a story adds flexibility to bedtime. Since you are not restricted by the text of a book, you can customize the stories by controlling the content and the length. If your young one exudes energy, start with an upbeat story that requires a good dose of interaction. Then switch to a quiet note with a soothing, gentle story that can be intertwined with a lullaby or a sweet melody. This will provide a nice transition between a busy schedule and the quiet, restful state needed to fall asleep.

Bedtime stories also give parents and children an opportunity to touch base and to bring closure to the day. Many children spend a good portion of their waking hours away from their parents. Even those who are at home are often engaged in their own activities. Stories based on the day's events are a good way to reconnect. This interlude provides one-on-one time without the distractions and interruptions that are part of a busy daytime schedule. When you put the book down, spinning a yarn becomes an intimate activity. With nothing between you and your child, direct eye contact and cuddling is easily accomplished. The warm, close feeling established by sharing a tale will send your child into slumber with a guarantee for sweet dreams.

There is no single recipe for perfect bedtime tales. All you need is imagination and a sense of humor. The only rule to follow is that the stories should be made up of the same ingredients as pleasant dreams. (Leave scary stories or those with heavy subject matter for a time when you and your child are awake enough to have a meaningful discussion.)

The direction that your story takes depends on your child. Does she like fantasy? Traditional tales? The familiar? When my older son was a pre-schooler he had a rich fantasy world. His days were filled with castles and trips to lands unknown. He was the perfect partner for a creative storytelling production. He would choose one or more characters and/or a location and then our imaginations would take over. A little bit of humor and a dose of the unbelievable was all that was necessary to pave his way to slumber. To ensure many nights of enjoyable listening, invent a character who can be followed on many adventures. My son and I invented "Pizzeria Lisa." Her culinary follies were endless.

My younger son is more of a realist. His most frequently requested story was "When I Was Born." He never got tired of that saga and eventually would help me tell it. He also enjoyed hearing and telling the stories that he had written during the day. (He drew the pictures and I took dictation.) Every time he told the story it changed and grew, the way a good story should.

Both of my children enjoyed family stories. We relived family outings to the zoo, apple orchard, and museums. They often completed the stories with details that I had forgotten. Anecdotes about extended family members gave them insight into the idiosyncratic ways of people they treasured. They especially enjoyed the funny vignettes that proved even adults can do silly things.

A classic story such as "The Three Bears" (or any folktale you remember from childhood) is another possibility for ending the day. As you tell the story, get inside it with your senses. Describe what you see, hear, and smell in order to "paint pictures" for your child, which she can complete with her imagination. Personalize the tale by substituting your child's name for one of the characters and adding facts from her life (names of relatives or friends, a favorite toy or activity, details about your home or neighborhood). To bring the story to life, create character voices, and let your child help provide sound effects.

So, when the lights are turned low and your child says, "tell me a story," don't grab a book. Just cuddle and let your imagination soar. As your child begins to drop off to sleep and her participation is limited to listening, finish the storytelling session with a summary of tomorrow's plans, a poem, or a lullaby. And be assured that you have provided the fuel for sweet, gentle dreams.

*Naomi Leithold, of Skokie, IL, is an award-winning storyteller, early childhood educator and author. She leads workshops for parents and teachers in storytelling techniques and literacy-related topics. Naomi has authored articles and audio reviews for national and local publications, and a book, **Oodles of Storytelling Ideas for the Early Childhood Classroom**. www.simplystorytelling.com*

Child Development: Ages and Stages

by Rebecca Isbell

A storyteller is sharing "The Three Billy Goats Gruff" with a group of children who range in age from three to twelve. The storyteller describes a horrible troll coming from under a rickety bridge. She makes a grotesque face and declares loudly, "Who's that trip-trapping on my bridge?" A young audience member begins to cry. An elementary school child is concerned about the goats. A twelve-year-old makes troll sounds with his friends. How could one story segment produce so many different responses? These children are reacting in different ways because of their differing levels of development and understanding.

Infants/Toddlers (Birth to Age 3)

Today, infants are recognized as active learners who are making thousands of connections in their brains. During the first three years, infants and toddlers learn through interactions with objects and people as they construct knowledge. This is the sensory-motor stage.[1]

In the area of social emotional development, Erik Erikson[2] identified the infant period as trust versus mistrust. Babies need a consistent and responsive person who meets their need for nourishment, love, and interaction. In a responsive environment, the infant learns that his needs will be met when he cries for food or comfort.

Toddlers (ages one to three) are establishing their autonomy as separate and independent people. They want to do things for themselves, even if they don't have the necessary skills. They need to be encouraged to be independent and try new things.

During the first three years of life, infants and toddlers are storing language away for future use. They need to be talked with and read to by adults, thereby helping them gain a rich understanding of words, conversational flow, and books.[3]

Stories and finger plays that invite children's involvement demonstrate to them that language is enjoyable and participatory. They are able to follow action-filled stories with sound effects and props. They may be frightened by grotesque faces and loud noises.

Pre-schoolers (Ages 3-5)

The pre-school years are a period of rapid development in all domains: intellectual, social/emotional, and physical. In the preoperational stage, young children learn by participating in concrete experiences such as going to a library or a petting zoo. Play is a major component of their learning; they experiment with toys and props. In play, pre-school children emulate what they have experienced. They begin to role-play and take on the characteristics of the people (or stories) in their environment. In the housekeeping center, a little boy may read to a baby doll the way his Daddy reads to his baby sister.

Language explodes as children progress from using a few words to using thousands. They ask questions: "What's that?" "Why?" "Where are we going?" A responsive adult helps children add to their growing language collection. Pre-schoolers enjoy repeating phrases, sounds, and stories. Revisiting stories assists them in story comprehension and in learning narrative structure. Although pre-schoolers are very verbal, they do not understand the difference between reality and fantasy. They are egocentric, so they believe everything in the story will happen to them.

Concrete Operations (Ages 6-12)

Six- and seven-year-old children are moving into the stage of concrete operations, although the transition varies from child to child. Once in the concrete stage, children are able to reason that although five pennies looks like more money, a dime is actually more valuable. Learning is still built on personal experiences, even with the onset of abstract thinking. Six- to twelve-year-olds are beginning to play games and conform to rules. They are interested in knowing if things "really happened" or if the story is "true."

As children begin school, they start to focus on mastering life skills. They learn to adapt to the school environment, compare themselves to others, and use the tools of their environment (reading, writing, math, etc.) During this process, school-age children establish a view of themselves as either industrious or inferior. Their self-esteem is built on their perceived achievements in comparison to others'. It is important to help them identify strengths without emphasizing their mistakes.

Language development continues to grow when children participate in interesting experiences, meaningful conversations, and image-rich stories. There is a wide range of abilities in this stage, from children with less complex language to children who have extensive vocabularies and are masterful communicators. The latter will begin to tell their own stories using the structure they have internalized. Significant differences also exist between the language competencies of a six-year-old and a twelve-year-old. Most twelve-year-olds are fluent speakers and communicate with an ease similar to that of an adult. They are able to tell detailed stories and often create original ones.

Formal Operational Thought

Somewhere between ages eleven and fifteen, most children move into Piaget's last stage of cognitive development, the period of formal operational thought. This stage is marked by the ability to think logically about abstract problems and to understand the general principles behind solutions to problems. They are able to imagine possibilities outside their realm of experience. Not all people reach this stage. Psychologists believe that accomplishing this depends on physical maturity and social and environmental experiences, including educational opportunities.

During childhood, many changes occur that influence how a child interprets and responds to a narrative. The storyteller who understands these developmental patterns will be better able to enrich the lives of children with appropriate and effective stories.

Notes

1. J. Piaget. *The Origins of Intelligence in Children*. NY: International Universities Press, 1952.
2. E. H. Erikson. *Childhood and Society*. NY: Norton, 1963.
3. L .S. Vygotsky. *Mind in Society: The Development of Higher Psychological Process*. Cambridge, MA: Harvard University Press, 1978.

Other Resources

Bee, H. *The Developing Child*. Menior Park, CA: Addison-Wesley, 1997.

Berk, L. *Infants, Children and Adolescents*. Boston: Allyn & Bacon, 1996.

Dr. Rebecca Isbell is Director of the Center of Excellence in Early Childhood Learning and Development and Professor of Early Childhood Education at East Tennessee State University. She is the author of eight books related to children including **Tell it Again** and **Tell it Again 2**, Beltsville, MD: Gryphon House, 1999 & 2000, both Parents' Choice Award recipients. Isbell@ETSU.edu

Selecting Age Appropriate Stories

by Judy Sima

In selecting stories, first and foremost, for any age, choose a story that appeals to you. If you like it, you'll enjoy sharing it with children. For young children you may need to simplify the story and add participation and gestures. For older children or adults, you may want to add more dialogue, description, and detail, and tone down the movements.

Pre-schoolers love stories with action, repetition, music, and participation. Choose stories with simple plots and few characters, unless the extra characters add sequentially to the repeated action. All children enjoy stories about boys and girls their own age. Find stories where little kids are the heroes. Stories should be non-violent. Simple fables and stories with animal characters work well, especially when children are allowed to act out the parts or make noises.

Suggestions: Three Bears, Three Little Pigs, Little Red Hen, The Lion and the Mouse, The Gingerbread Man, The Gunniwolf (Wilhelmina Harper), Caps for Sale (Esphyr Slobodkina), Millions of Cats (Wanda Gág)

Early elementary children (ages 5-7) also enjoy repetition and participation, but they can appreciate stories with a more detailed story line. This age group likes clear, definite answers. Good triumphs over evil. The villain is eliminated. Don't sweeten the ending by having the wicked witch or wolf run off; the children may fear that the villain will return and "get" them. These youngsters also love stories about kids like themselves who get into trouble. Simple, obvious, and slapstick humor works well. Scary stories with funny endings are a huge hit.

Suggestions: Little Red Riding Hood, Bremen Town Musicians, The Old Woman Who Lived in a Vinegar Bottle, The Great Big Enormous Turnip, Rumpelstiltskin, Boo Baby Girl Meets the Ghost of Mable's Gable (Jim May), Thomas' Snow Suit (Robert Munsch),

Something from Nothing (Phoebe Gilman), Joseph Had a Little Overcoat (Simms Taback), Tikki Tikki Tembo (Arlene Mosel), Anansi and the Moss Covered Rock (Eric Kimmel), The Little Old Lady Who Wasn't Afraid of Anything (Linda Williams), Too Much Noise (Ann McGovern), Ira Sleeps Over (Bernard Waber)

Middle grade children (ages 8-10) enjoy longer, more intricate folktales, classic scary stories, tall tales, how and why stories, and humorous stories with surprise endings. This audience will sit longer and fidget less, but still enjoy participating or acting out parts of the story.

Suggestions: Snow White, Lazy Jack, The Steadfast Tin Soldier, Paul Bunyan, John Henry, How the Spider Got His Small Waist, Stone Soup, The Golden Arm, The Three Wishes, It Could Always Be Worse (Margot Zemach), Lon Po Po (Ed Young), Why Mosquitoes Buzz in People's Ears (Verna Aardema), Wiley and the Hairy Man (Molly Bang), Who Took My Hairy Toe? (Shutta Crum), Tailypo (Paul Galdone), Rough Faced Girl (Rafe Martin)

Middle school students (ages 11-14) love to be scared, grossed out, challenged, entertained, and treated like adults, but don't expect much of a reaction from this age group. They will participate on a limited basis once you've won them over. Eye contact may be difficult for them, and they are painfully aware of fitting in with their peers. Look for myths, legends, tall tales, real ghost stories, urban legends, trickster tales, and historical stories. Strong lessons are okay, too, but let listeners figure them out for themselves.

Suggestions: Mr. Fox, Sir Gawain and the Loathly Lady, King Arthur, The Lion's Whisker (Nancy Raines Day), The Cowtail Switch (Harold Courlander), Mary Culhane (Molly Bang), Tatterhood (Ethel Johnston Phelps), The Stonecutter (Gerald McDermott), The Boy Who Drew Cats (Arthur A. Levine), The First Strawberries (Joseph Bruchac) For something a little more challenging, try short stories from authors Neil Shusterman: *Mind Storms: Stories to Blow Your Mind* or Paul Jennings: *Unreal, Uncovered, Uncanny, and Unmentionable.*

Where to Look

Visit the children's section of your local public library. In most libraries, folktales, fairy tales, legends, and tall tales can be found in the section beginning with 398. Bible stories are located in the 220s and mythology can be found beginning with 290. Because they were written for children, these stories appeal to young people and are usually age appropriate.

Check the picture book and easy reader sections. Try reading picture books without looking at the illustrations. Many beautifully illustrated books are just too wordy for storytelling. Other picture books rely on the illustrations to tell the story. You may have to adapt the story by condensing or embellishing the text. Add a rhyme, a song, repetition, or participation to make the story come alive.

Ask the children's librarian at the public library or contact a nearby school media specialist. These professionals are trained to work with young people and know their interests. They are happy to help you. You might even receive an invitation to practice your tales in the library or school. Haunt used bookstores and library book sales for old picture books and folktale collections. Many of the out of print books have wonderful, long forgotten tales you can bring to life again. Watch other storytellers, not to "steal" their stories, but to learn what stories work with different ages. Observe how tellers engage the children and how they bring stories to life.

Finally, become a child yourself. Develop a sense of joy and wonder; enjoy, play, laugh, and revel in the tales. Children will forgive even a poor choice of story if they know you love and respect them, and they will appreciate a well-chosen tale all the more.

Judy Sima is a retired school librarian, free-lance storyteller, and widely published author of articles on storytelling. She has presented workshops across the country, contributed to NSN's *Beginner's Guide to Storytelling*, and coauthored, with Kevin Cordi, a 2004 Storytelling World Honor Book, *Raising Voices: Creating Youth Storytelling Groups and Troupes*. judy@judysima.com

Making Story Magic:
Developing a Storytelling Program

by Dianne de Las Casas

Creating a solid children's storytelling program involves many considerations. The age and experience of the audience, the telling environment, the choice and flow of the material, and the overall length of the program should all be examined. A well-planned, well-performed program makes "story magic."

Age Levels and Background

In schools, children are usually grouped by grades – for example, K-3 or 4-6, so that stories can be geared directly to those ages. Mixed groups, such as library audiences, require stories that appeal to all age levels. Library audiences in particular often include children younger than recommended because parents bring young siblings along with the children in the target age group.

You will need stories that incorporate subtle adult humor as well as kid-friendly fare for family audiences. Folktale collections are excellent places to find stories that appeal to a wide age range. It's good to have extra selections at your disposal, too, in case the ages aren't what you expected and you need to adjust your program on the spot.

Consider the life experience of your audience. Children in the city may respond differently from suburban or rural listeners. For example, a group of urban pre-schoolers may not know what a billy goat looks like and a short explanation may be needed.

Children love references to the familiar: learn about their class, their neighborhood, the books they read, and even their favorite TV shows.

Performance Environments

In situations with lots of potential distractions, such as outdoor venues, plan short, simple tales and a variety of songs, games, or story stretches. For large audiences, be sure to build in extra time to focus listeners between pieces. Plan for a sound system if needed. Smaller spaces may call for more intimate stories.

Themes

You may want to weave a common thread through your program to create a theme. Educators, librarians, and presenters appreciate themes because they tie in with curricula or special events. Holidays, curricular material, historical events (e.g., the California Gold Rush), cultural or ethnic themes are all possibilities. Themes help focus a program – but be sure your chosen thread lends itself to a wide enough range of stories for a varied program.

Openings, Closings, and Segues

The presenter may offer to introduce your program. If so, supply her with an introduction card. If you are introducing yourself, provide fun or funny facts. A simple, brief introduction is best.

One of the openings I use (after being introduced) is a chant I wrote: "No matter how near, no matter how far / Stories are magic wherever you are." I chant the first half by myself, teach the kids the second half, and they recite their part in response to mine. I sometimes use this as a transition between stories, as well. A short poem, a song, or a personal anecdote may also serve as a good beginning to a story session.

Prepare for bridges between stories: narrative introductions, story games, poems, chants, or songs. (See "Intros, Outros, and Story Stretches" by Naomi Baltuck.) Perhaps you need to elevate the audience's energy after a sad story. Or maybe you want to refocus your listeners after a raucous, funny tale. These "story stretches" cleanse the palate between story entrees and prepare the listeners for the next course.

How will you leave your listeners? Sometimes a show's opening can bring the program full circle and serve as the closing. Or a line about how the listeners can now share the stories with others may be appropriate. Many performers thank their audience and compliment them on their listening skills. Others bring giveaways such as bookmarks, which they enlist attending adults in distributing at the end of the show. Check your host's policy on giveaway items. Be sure to have enough for everyone and know how they will be delivered.

Pacing, Flow, and Length

Your program should keep your listeners engaged through-out while allowing them time to process each story. It should include a variety of story types, some quiet and lyrical, others funny and perhaps with movement and sound effects. It should build toward a climax and then end with a finale – one that will leave the kids exhilarated but not overly excited.

In a typical 45-minute program, I generally include an introduction, three or four stories with stretches between them, and a closing song. Start with a story that will capture your audience's attention. Many audiences are initially hesitant about joining in. Your audience needs time to get to know and trust you. For instance, in my "Jump, Jiggle and Jam" program, I begin with a modernized version of "The Little Red Hen." Beginning the program with a familiar story helps the audience feel comfortable.

Tell longer or more challenging stories in the second or third slot on the program. The audience knows you by now, and you have connected with them. In my "Jambalaya" show, the second story I tell is "Pullin' Up the Sweet Potato," a Louisiana version of the Russian folktale "The Gigantic Turnip." The story employs several volunteers onstage and engages the whole audience in vigorous participation. Know your stories' personalities and think about where they would best fit in your program.

Parents and teachers appreciate it when the kids leave your performance feeling great but not too hyped up. A song or a poem brings the energy down to manageable levels, perhaps summarizing the theme of your program. I often end with a song that everyone can sing together. For example, in "Across America," I end with the song "This Land is Your Land" and have several children join me onstage playing rhythm instruments.

Begin and end your show on time. Classes or other activities may be scheduled around your performance. Most children's storytelling programs run 30-45 minutes – shorter for younger audiences, longer for older ones. Be sure to time your show so that you know it will fit within the scheduled time slot.

Making Story Magic

Whatever you choose to tell, your characters, settings, pronunciations, and cultural, historical, or scientific facts should all be well-researched. When telling stories with lessons, avoid moralizing and allow your listeners to draw their own conclusions.

Finally, practice your storytelling as often as possible – by yourself, with friends and family, with story coaches, and with formal and informal audiences. Fine tune and adjust your programs. Try out a new story along with your "tried and true" tales, the ones that you already know will work. Test new ways of telling old favorites. Most importantly, listen to your listeners and make story magic wherever you are.

***Dianne de Las Casas** is an award-winning storyteller and author who tours internationally. Her performances, "traditional folklore gone fun," are full of energetic audience participation. A leader in the arts community, de Las Casas has co-founded several arts organizations and is a Louisiana Touring Directory Artist. www.storyconnection.net*

Practice, Practice, Practice

by Betty Lehrman

The old joke goes, "How do you get to Carnegie Hall?" The answer: "Practice, practice, practice." But practicing a story is serious business. Thorough rehearsal can mean the difference between a carefree, playful, confident performance and one fraught with difficulty.

Learning a story usually *doesn't* mean memorizing a text. It is very difficult to memorize words and then imbue them with enough meaning that an audience will happily come along for the ride. Besides, storytelling is a conversation between teller and audience – a good teller will be open to playing with that interaction, bending the story to suit the audience's reactions. Of course, if you are telling a Dr. Seuss story or an epic poem, you may want to memorize it, in which case you'll want to know the words so well that you can still play with characterization, pacing, timing, and emphasis.

Relating a story is like telling about a memory or reliving a movie with your listeners. We want the audiences to see the images in their heads. We want to introduce them to the emotions, the settings, and the events which drive the characters and the plot. I hate rehearsing. But in the twenty-five years I've told stories professionally, I've learned a variety of useful rehearsal techniques. Find the ones which work for you.

Learning the Story

- First, tell *about* the story. What draws you to it? What does it mean? What is its essence?
- Outline the story. Write down the sequence of scenes in order. Or write a short synopsis of the plot.
- Explore the characters. Find a voice and stance, facial expression or movement for each main character.
- Develop a script or a detailed outline. If you are adapting a folktale, write down your adaptation. If you are

working from a text (and have gotten permission to tell it – necessary in anything other than a strictly educational setting), read it out loud. Include phrases or expressions which particularly add to the story. Keep making notes as you work.

- Tell the story into a tape recorder. If you have a script, try telling the story without reading it. Then follow the script as you listen to the recording. What did you leave out that is important? Note it down. Tape it again.

- Listen to your taped story. Take the recording with you – either the one you read, or the one you told. Listen to it in the car, around the house, in bed before you fall asleep. I often listen to tapes of past performances when I am on my way to a gig.

- Establish the first and last lines and specific dialogue. You may want to memorize these. The first line sets the scene and jogs the teller's memory. The dialogue helps you stay in touch with your characters and their intentions. The last line gives a sense of completion; being sure of it guarantees that you are leaving your audience with exactly the feeling you want.

Rehearsals

Turn off the phone, close the door, and let the laundry lie there. Tell the story – to yourself, to your dog, to your wall. Tell it in front of a mirror. Tell it into a tape recorder again. (That always keeps me focused and unlikely to stop in the middle to vacuum.) Tell it to yourself while you are exercising – I once learned a 70-minute narrative over a period of weeks while swimming laps.

Pay attention to the characters in the story. Are they well-drawn? Too much? The characters speak to each other: the giant must look down, while Jack looks way, way up. When are you the narrator, telling to the children? When are you speaking in character, and to whom? The clearer you are about who you are portraying at any moment, the more effortlessly your audience will see the tale unfold.

Establish where scenery and objects are located in space as you tell. "See" the scenes and place them somewhere in front of you. Be consistent: the kitchen is always on the right; the wheat field is always in the distance. If you are miming an object, be aware of its weight, when you touch it, when you release it (let it go), and where you put it when you are finished with it.

Then go for a live audience: your mother, your neighbor, your kids, a rehearsal buddy; whoever will listen. If you know another storyteller in your area, trade rehearsal times with each other. Read the faces of your listeners: are they with you? Are they bored? Will they laugh happily if you purse your lips or pause just a fraction of a second longer? Will they tune you out if you milk the tragedy for too long? Follow your listeners' reactions to find the humor and the pathos. Note how you may change the story for younger or older listeners.

Then: breathe deeply, go forth and tell. See you at Carnegie Hall.

> **Betty Lehrman** writes, directs plays, and tells
> stories from her home in Framingham, MA.
> www.bettylehrman.com

Proper
Prior Planning
by Linda Gorham

My father used to say, "Proper prior planning prevents poor performance." I have found this to be wise advice for living and even wiser for running my storytelling business.

There is no greater joy than sharing a story with a young person. It is magical. But "proper prior planning" creates that magic; it does not happen on its own. It's more than simply selecting the right stories. We've got to meet the goals of the hiring venue, be in the right space, have the right sound system, earn a satisfactory amount of money, and make sure we communicate well with our host.

Gathering Facts

The phone rings. The caller wants a teller for a group of children. And he or she is interested in you! So far, so good. First, gather some facts. To avoid missing pertinent information, I designed inquiry/assignment sheets. They are bright pink; I keep them near my phone. The color makes them easy to spot, and they become the first page for my pending or assignment files. They have room for all of the necessary info: proposed date, time, length of program, contact name, address, fax, phone and email info, and referral source. Plus, they have spaces for the address and location of the show and the stories planned.

What Do They Really Want?

Before I get too detailed, I need to find out what callers *really* want and whom they want it for. I ask questions: Who is the decision maker? What does he or she want to accomplish? Should the program tie into the curriculum or a school or summer theme, or must it meet the requirements of a grant? Is this program related to a holiday or special celebration? Are there particular stories or story types required? How many children are expected and in what age range? The more I know, the better.

I try to be part of the event planning process. My task is to see if there is a good match between what the sponsor wants and what I am willing to provide. If the type of program requested is not for me, I tell this to callers. Often I can recommend another teller. Either way I have an opportunity to develop a rapport with callers. Every connection provides potential for employment – even if it is at another time.

Location, Location, Location

The location makes a huge difference. Ideally, I'd like a room that is comfortably full without too much extra space, has no traffic from passersby, and has no visual or auditory distractions (find out if bells will ring and never tell in front of a window). Typically, I'll be offered gyms, lunchrooms, auditoriums, multipurpose rooms, or outside spaces.

Gyms have horrible acoustics, but there is plenty of room. For young children, I try to have them sit on the floor. Chairs create barriers. Bleachers are disasters waiting to happen: they are spread out, noisy, and potentially dangerous.

Auditoriums are better. The sound is usually good and it is easy to manage larger groups. There is one drawback: often the stage is too far away from the audience. In that case I ask for steps to be added center stage so that during the show I can occasionally move closer to the audience. One plus: where I limit gym and multipurpose groups to a maximum of 300, I'll allow up to 500 students in an auditorium. Fixed chairs and an elevated stage do make a difference.

Meeting rooms in libraries are usually pretty good spaces. Multipurpose rooms and lunchrooms are probably the most popular venues for elementary school performances. But remember, the lunchroom staff will need time to set up and/or break down tables. My rule: no tables during a show. Tables are barriers to an intimate experience. *(Yes, telling to 300 kids can be intimate!)*

And now, on to my least favorite venue: the great outdoors. My voice will blow like the wind and I will invariably encounter the distractions of the world. I've had to compete with giant inflated jumping rooms, a fire truck loaded with firemen who started tearing down a nearby building, and a helicopter that landed behind me. Even the best stories can't compete!

A "Sound" Investment

The best investment I ever made was in my sound system. Without one, I was at the mercy of schools that had marginal to awful systems, if they had anything at all. I was once offered a bullhorn! Bad sound will translate into a bad performance. I recommend a system with a wireless lavaliere (a small mike which pins on a shirt) or a headset – my favorite – for unencumbered hands and freedom of movement.

Negotiating Fees

Storytelling is an art worthy of a respectable wage. Negotiating fees is tricky because there are no hard and fast rules. I need to feel that my time and efforts are valued, but I don't want to price myself out of the market. In determining your fees, consider the following:

- Your experience level
- Potential to build your reputation (is the venue prestigious? what publicity might you get?)
- Fees other local tellers are charging
- Sponsoring group's budget *(it is okay to ask)*
- Travel time
- New stories that may have to be developed
- Personal affiliation with the venue or audience

Efficiency is Key

I developed a contract form on my computer into which I simply type the important details discussed above. I send a cover letter and two copies of the contract (I keep a third copy). I request that one contract be signed and returned to me with directions. I also send a sheet outlining my space and set-up requirements, plus a publicity notice that the venue can use for advertising my show. And I send every job a thank you letter. Someone took the time to hire me; I take the time to say thanks.

Ask Questions, Offer Input, and Confirm Details

I try not to sound like a census taker, but building the "who, what, where, and why" questions into my initial conversations has saved me many headaches. I feel prepared, I understand my audience's needs, and I'll be in the best possible location. Then I relax. Now, on to the stories!

Linda Gorham tours nationally. In 2003 she co-chaired the National Storytelling Conference in Chicago. In 2004 she co-led a group of sixty-two American storytellers who traveled to South Africa as part of a professional exchange. Linda is a founding member of ASE: The Chicago Association of Black Storytellers and an award-winning recording artist. www.LindaGorham.com

Intros, Outros, and Story Stretches

by Naomi Baltuck

Want to inject some positive energy into your storytelling programs? Try "story stretching" your repertoire. A story stretch is any song, chant, poem, joke, riddle, participation story, or tongue twister that actively engages an audience. A stretch can serve as a snappy opener or conclude a program on just the right note, add balance and variety to a show, or raise or lower the energy level of a group. It can complement a theme, help your audience "shake the ants out of its pants," or simply be spontaneous fun. Best of all, whether you are being playful or singing a thoughtful song, whether telling to pre-schoolers or high schoolers, a story stretch is the quickest way to build rapport with your audience.

For a fun, rowdy story stretch, try the song "My Aunt Came Back."[1] The audience repeats each line after the leader sings it, and mirrors the leader's actions.

Leader: My aunt came back
Group: My aunt came back
Leader: From old Japan
Group: From old Japan
Leader: And brought with her
Group: And brought with her
Leader: A lovely fan *(wave hand back & forth in fanning motion)*
Group: A lovely fan

The song continues with additional places the aunt returned from (e.g., "the county fair") and rhyming items ("and brought with her . . . a rocking chair"), each verse with accompanying action. Each motion, once started, is continued. Soon the audience is fanning, rocking, yo-yoing, chewing, and woggling their heads all at once. The cumulative effect is hilarious!

Stretches are "storytelling candy" – delicious fun in one quick bite. Every teller should have at least a few of these sweet treats to pull out of her bag of tricks. Just keep in mind a few rules of thumb:

- Keep stretches age appropriate. With a mixed audience, "stretch" the younger kids with a slightly more challenging selection rather than risk losing the older kids' interest.

- Keep directions simple. If it takes longer to teach than to sing or play, it's probably not worth your time.

- Tune in to your audience. If they seem bored or restless, the material is probably too easy, too difficult, or too long.

- Challenge your audience. Whether children are making crazy hand motions, attempting a tongue twister, or inventing their own verses, they will enjoy rising to the occasion.

- Keep the pace comfortable. If a learned skill is required, as when you are teaching a clapping game or a tongue-tangling chorus, let your audience learn at a comfortable pace, then bring them up to speed.

- Stretch yourself! Be dramatic, be silly, let yourself go.

- Avoid negative comments. If the audience response is slow, say, "Let's try that one more time to be sure that everyone has it." If they are reticent about participating, don't take it personally. Some kids might be too young or too "cool" to join in, but they will still enjoy listening and watching. It's okay to fill in the blanks yourself, drop the echo, or tell a story without help on the chants, as long as you keep up your energy and enthusiasm.

- Be clear as to what you expect. When you introduce a stretch, begin by singing a verse so that the group can hear the melody or rhythm. Some stretches are so easy, a nod of encouragement is all it takes for kids to mirror your movements or join in on the chorus. Others require a formal invitation such as: "Do you remember how the chorus goes?" "Snap your fingers and help me get a good beat going!" or "Will you be my echo? I'll sing a line to you, and you sing it right back."

- Open with something warm and compelling. This breaks the ice and welcomes listeners into your story world. I like Shel Silverstein's poem, "Invitation,"[2] which begins, "If you are a dreamer, come in . . . " I also open with "Little Rap Riding Hood[3]," which is fresh and funny and a crowd pleaser for all ages. Save your most energetic activities for the middle of a program, when your audience will really appreciate that seventh inning stretch. For the "home stretch," wind down the energy level with something sweet or thoughtful, such as "Pass It On" or "Mmm, I Want to Linger," both described in *Crazy Gibberish* (see below.) This will gently return listeners to the real world and send them home still feeling connected.

- For a single session, go with tried-and-true favorites. Echo songs are fool-proof; call and response songs are dynamic; a knock-knock joke is always good for a laugh. When working with the same group over an extended period of time, the first session is still the most important: use your strongest material and the kids will eagerly anticipate the next session. Over the course of your visits, you and your group can build a collective repertoire including more complicated stretches.

- Keep records of your stretches. Make a video or audio recording to document the words, melody, and motions, so that you will not forget them, even after periods of disuse.

No matter what stories you tell, or to whom, by any "stretch of the imagination," you have at your fingertips the means to actively engage your listeners, by the hand and by the heart.

Notes

1. Naomi Baltuck. *Crazy Gibberish and Other Story Hour Stretches*. New Haven, CT: Linnet Books, 1993.
2. Shel Silverstein. *Where the Sidewalk Ends*. NY: Harper & Row, 1974.
3. Naomi Baltuck. *Crazy Gibberish*.

Other Recommended Resources

Cobb, Jane. *I'm a Little Teapot: Presenting Preschool Storytime.* Vancouver, B.C: Black Sheep Press, 2001.

MacDonald, Margaret Read. *Shake-It-Up Tales!* Little Rock, AR: August House, 2000.

Schwartz, Alvin. *A Twister of Twists, a Tangler of Tongues.* Philadelphia: J.B. Lippincott, 1972.

Tashjian, Virginia. *Juba this and Juba That.* Boston: Little, Brown and Company, 1969. Also: *With a Deep Sea Smile.* 1974.

Winn, Marie. *The Fireside Book of Fun and Games.* NY: Schuster, 1974.

Withers, Carl and Sula Benet. *Riddles of Many Lands.* NY: Abelard-Schuman, 1956.

*Naomi Baltuck of Edmonds, WA has written and produced numerous award-winning books and CDs. Her book **Apples From Heaven** (Shoestring Press, 1995) received the Anne Izard Storytellers' Choice and three Storytelling World Awards. Naomi presents storytelling workshops and performances throughout the USA. nbaltuck@earthlink.net*

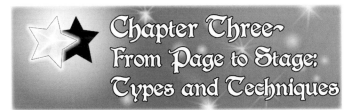

Once Upon a Time, Long Ago:
Finding and Adapting Folktales

by Margaret H. Lippert

With their rollicking language and universal themes, folktales are perfect stories to tell wherever you have a few quiet moments with children. Honed by generations of telling and countless tellers, folktales deepen children's awareness of story structure and enrich their vocabulary while providing new perspectives on human behavior and cultures around the world, past and present. And . . . folktales are fun!

Folktales are stories that have been passed orally from one person to another, and therefore have no single author. They include fairy tales (which have an element of magic or transformation), legends, tall tales, myths, and fables.

Finding Folktales

You probably know many folktales without reference to printed sources – "The Three Bears," "Hansel and Gretel," and "The Three Billy Goats Gruff" are all familiar. However, when it comes to finding and learning folktales to present, the task can seem daunting. Your local library, the Internet, and bookstores all contain excellent resources.

The 398.2 section of the library is the mother lode of folktales and folklore. I like collections of stories by storytellers for storytellers, such as those by Margaret Read MacDonald, Joe Hayes or Diane Wolkstein. These stories are retold with an ear for oral presentation. Other collections may be useful, as well, but may require more adaptation before they work as tales for telling.

You can also research stories on-line. Using a search engine like Google, look up specific folklore subjects (e.g., "folktale lions"), themes ("folktale quest"), or geographical areas ("folktales Africa"). This will lead you to story texts and endless links to related sites with still more stories.

Another avenue is to browse through the children's section of bookstores to find newly published books or recordings. Authors like Baba Wagué Diakité, Jane Yolen, and Judy Sierra have all published fabulous books based on folktales. Recordings by Cathy Spagnoli, Lynn Moroney, and Bobby Norfolk will give you a feel for oral cadences and vocal possibilities.

However, you need to be careful using copyrighted work. Teachers or parents may use copyrighted material in an educational or family setting without a problem. But if you are a storyteller-for-hire, you need to use material that is in the public domain, get permission from the author or teller to use his version of the story, or develop your own adaptation of a folktale.

Material in the public domain is that which is no longer copyrighted, and therefore available for use. It is difficult to know whether or not a folktale is protected by copyright, but if it was published over 75 years ago or if there are three or more published versions of it, it is probably in the public domain. Copyright laws are described in more detail at www.copyright.gov.

Many authors will give permission for their original stories or folktale adaptations to be told. Contact the writer or teller directly (through his website, for example), or write the permissions department of the publisher. And even if you are telling in volunteer, educational, or non-public situations, you should always give credit to the source. When I am telling a folktale from a collection or from a picture book, I always bring the book to show the audience.

In developing your own version of a folktale, find at least two or three interpretations of the tale and take some elements from each. You may enjoy dipping into *The Storyteller's Sourcebook: A Subject, Title, and Motif Index to Folklore Collections for Children* by

Margaret Read MacDonald (Thomson Gale, Pub., 1982) or *The Storyteller's Sourcebook 1983-1999 Supplement* by MacDonald and Brian W. Sturm (Gale, 2001).

A storytelling recording represents the teller's unique voice and her particular account of the tale. It is not ethical to memorize a storyteller's performance and use it as your own. A detailed statement on storytelling etiquette, particularly concerning telling other storytellers' spoken versions of tales, is included in *A Beginner's Guide to Storytelling* (National Storytelling Network, 2003).

Adapting Folktales

Many times I find a story that I like that isn't perfect for my needs. It may have elements that attract me but it is too long, too complex, or the language does not flow smoothly. In these cases I locate several versions of the folktale, read them all through, close the books, and create my own version. I focus on plot, language, character, humor, and setting.

List the major scenes. Ask yourself if they follow a clear pattern. If there are scenes that seem tangential, eliminate or condense them to improve the flow. Keep the conflict and resolution clear.

Look for rhythmic language and opportunities for different sounds. If there is music or dancing in a story, add words, movement, a tune, or all three. When I tell a story about a turtle who plays the flute, I play a bamboo flute and repeat the tune throughout the story. Children love the rhythmic refrain from one of the Dan stories I tell from Liberia: *Kokoloko, Dukoloko, Chay, chay, chay*.

Identify the qualities of the characters and infuse your telling with these. Add dialogue, gestures, or movement to convey a sense of wiliness, sloth, or wisdom. If there are animal characters in the story, play with animal sounds and characteristic voices.

Many stories benefit from humor – in word play, character-izations, or unexpected events. If there are places you can insert humorous elements, try them. They may become treasured moments.

Remember the setting. This element is often missing from folktales in collections, yet it is important to share clues that will let your listeners know where and when the story takes place. Just mentioning a palm tree or a blackberry bush may help the audience relax into the surroundings and join you in the imagined place.

Amid all your tinkering with the story, remember the underlying message. Is it about overcoming pain, dealing with adversity, sustaining hope, or caring for others? After I have adjusted the story for the elements listed above, I always ask myself, "Did I retain the heart of the story?"

Onward!

Finding, developing, and telling folktales is a great way to invigorate yourself and your listeners. When I was a classroom teacher, I told a folktale every Friday afternoon to send students off for the weekend with a story gift. Teachers, parents, and childcare workers have ready audiences and a multitude of opportunities in which to tell folktales for fun and learning. So, go for it. "Once upon a time, long ago . . . "

*Margaret (Meg) H. Lippert, Ed. D., has taught in Tanzania and Guatemala, at Columbia University's Teachers College, and at Bank Street College of Education. She currently teaches at the University of Washington. A professional storyteller since 1970, Meg has published twenty-one books of folktales, including, with Won-Ldy Paye, **Mrs. Chicken and the Hungry Crocodile** (NY: Henry Holt, 2003). www.storypower.net*

Personal and Historical Stories

by Betty Lehrman

I have always been a fan of historical fiction, delighting in Sidney Taylor's *All of a Kind Family*, Esther Forbes's *Johnny Tremain*, and the literary forays of Louisa May Alcott. And I loved to listen to my grandmother's stories of her childhood in Russia. But as I entered the storytelling world, I found that most of the material I heard, or performed myself, was from folktales rather than history or real life.

In the mid 1980s Kel Watkins, a storyteller from Australia, shared an autobiographical tale onstage at the National Storytelling Festival. I breathed the dry dust with him, heard the animal sounds of the Outback . . . I felt I had walked through a sensory window into another world. He was sharing a personal tale from his childhood – I could do that!

I had already worked as a storyteller for several years. Why, I thought, should I continue to deal with adapting stories from multiple sources, or securing permissions of others' copyrighted material, when I could tell my own stories from personal experience? What could be easier?

Developing historical and autobiographical stories proved to have its own challenges. Folktales have universal themes, recognizable characters, and neatly sewn-up endings. With personal and historical tales, a teller has to pick and choose the appropriate elements and craft a well-structured, satisfying story which resonates with a wide audience.

I use short personal anecdotes frequently in performance, mostly to introduce longer stories and songs. "Have you ever been afraid of the dark?" I ask. "Of monsters? Of something under your bed?" The children nod seriously; hands go up to indicate they have. "Of the *refrigerator*?" The audience laughs and I tell how I was afraid of the sound of the refrigerator motor in the middle of the night. Then I go on to tell a scary folktale or sing a funny song about a little girl and the alligator under her bed. Anecdotes are wonderful in connecting listeners to the speaker.

Crafting longer personal or historical stories takes time, distance, and a critical eye for structure. Personal stories need to serve the audience, not provide therapy for the teller. Real life doesn't flow like a well-told tale, and endings are the most difficult to construct – they are seldom neat. I found that I needed distance from events or people in order to see them in perspective. For example, it took me several years after my grandmother died to write a story portrait of her. I needed time to digest our relationship and figure out how I wanted to remember her, and fit that into story form.

Stories must have a beginning, middle, and end with recognizable, sympathetic characters. They should develop a theme, come to a climax, and then gather together all of the loose ends. The best stories plant clues and images in the beginning which are referred to or developed by the end of the tale; they are circular. Repeated images, sounds, or phrases serve as touch points to keep an audience attentive.

I began working on "The Blue Shawl," now a 70-minute piece based on my grandmother's memoirs, with an unembellished story which my grandmother had written down in a few paragraphs. I knew it was a compelling incident, but I couldn't find a satisfying ending, and there was no climax. I remembered storyteller Donald Davis's advice: "Don't let the facts get in the way of the truth." I researched historical particulars and gathered as many factual details as I could, both to add to my grandmother's descriptions and to get a larger sense of the times. I rearranged characters and events. I rewrote the story multiple times over the course of many months until it felt right. I began performing it and made still more changes. It still follows the incident, with lots of family details, but it is no longer just my grandmother's tale. And I am careful to tell children (who always want to know) what "really" happened and what I changed or invented for the sake of the story.

Many wonderful performers, including Judith Black, Syd Lieberman, and Jay O'Callahan, have created engrossing stories which deal with historical events. Other performers portray

Abraham Lincoln, Ben Franklin, or Louisa May Alcott. Several years ago I decided to develop a purely historical piece. I looked for a well-known person who would tie in with elementary school curricula. I chose pioneer and author Laura Ingalls Wilder.

First, I spent several months on research. I read every book written by and about Mrs. Wilder. I joined a listserv and corresponded with diehard fans and scholars. I viewed videos and live shows. I visited the Wilder home and museum in Mansfield, Missouri. I compiled all the information I could until I was bursting with it. But what would be in my show?

I called in my rehearsal buddy. She listened as I followed my outline and told her the story of Wilder's life, in chronological order. She was bored. I needed to start over. "Begin when the status quo changes," I remembered from a workshop. I tried starting when the Ingalls family was about to move from Wisconsin to Minnesota. I roughly followed the events in Wilder's *On the Banks of Plum Creek*, but instead of sticking to the fictionalized book, I made the few necessary changes to follow the historically accurate record. Beginning with the move West, I told about the seasons, the new house, school, and the terrible grasshopper plague, and ended with reflecting back on "my" (Laura's) life.

I was almost ready. I had an interesting story told in character, but I hadn't tried it out yet, and I wasn't sure which form my planned audience participation would take. I volunteered to visit local elementary school classrooms. Once there, I experimented with different ways of introducing the show, telling the story, and soliciting and refining the audience participation. Afterwards, I asked for questions and noted what most interested the students. Next, I dry-mounted large posters of the Ingalls family, made costumes and a backdrop, and created a teacher kit with vocabulary and resource lists. I was ready to hit the road with a well-researched, well-developed, emotionally rich program.

Using personal and historical material – sharing one's own history or telling about other times, events, and people – can be extremely rewarding. Anecdotes about a teller's personal life draw listeners in, engaging them. They can serve as wonderful bridges between more developed tales. Longer stories should honor listeners with satisfying narratives. The mere fact that an event happened to the teller or his family is not reason enough for audiences to want to listen. Stories must be compelling on their own merit. Universal themes, clearly drawn characters, thorough research, and most of all, a solid structure are the keys to personal and historical tales well told.

Betty Lehrman has performed across the US, Thailand, and Australia since 1978. Winner of Parents' Choice and American Library Association awards, she was founding editor of the LANES (League for the Advancement of New England Storytelling) "Museletter." Betty is the drama director at the Benjamin Franklin Charter School (Franklin, MA) and at the Performing Arts Center of MetroWest in Framingham, MA. www.bettylehrman.com

Scary Stories: Balancing Fright with Delight

by Diane Ladley

What storyteller hasn't at some time slunk home after a Halloween gig, miserably certain she's psychologically scarred a child for life? You may vow that you'll never tell another ghost story again – but the fact remains that *children love ghost stories*. So it is up to you to ensure that your performance carefully balances fright with delight.

Understanding Fear in Children

Understanding fear in children – how it works, what frightens them, and at what age – is crucial to balancing fright with delight. According to Dozier's *Fear Itself* (St. Martin's Griffin, 1998), 15% of children are more fearful than average – but 30% are fearless! I begin telling ghost stories to children aged four and up. Do *not* tell ghost stories to children three and under.

Ages 4-6

Young children are very vulnerable to fear because they haven't yet developed a rational understanding of it. To adults, a child's fear may seem illogical, but to a youngster it's vivid and intense. Young children can't distinguish fantasy from reality. A terrified child *genuinely believes* a monster is in her closet ready to eat her.

The first human fears are of spiders, snakes, monsters, deep rumbling noises, man-eating animals, and fire. These primitive anxieties make sense when you realize that fear is a survival mechanism. Our cave-dwelling ancestors needed to be afraid of these things, for meeting up with any of them could spell death.

Ages 4-6 love good, giggly, ghostly fun. G-rated stories must always have a happy ending, leaving the children in an emotionally secure, comforting place. Highly interactive, get-'em-moving stories work well. Favorite tales are "Wait 'Til

Martin Comes" and "The Little Old Lady Who Wasn't Afraid of Anything" and songs like "Have You Seen the Ghost of John?"

Ages 7-12

Children learn to control their fears through experience and instruction. While fear of imaginary threats decreases, realistic fears increase, including those regarding personal safety. Ghost stories help children deal with rational fears; they teach children appropriate reactions when danger threatens. Scary stories present frightening scenarios (a zombie is coming after me!) and provide possible responses (I'll run, climb a tree, make a clever escape). This empowers children. Ghost stories are extremely beneficial to the development of an emotionally healthy child.

Tell PG-rated stories that teach survival and moral lessons to these children. The stories might not have happy endings, but they should feature heroes who face great danger and survive. Heroes are saved by their wits or by the goodness of their hearts, while the wicked are punished. Shivery folktales are perfect. Tell true ghost stories with caution. Stories should be comparable to R.L. Stine's *Goosebumps* books or the *Scooby-Doo* cartoons. Kids this age love stories like "The Golden Arm," "Milk Bottles," "Resurrection Mary," or "Mr. Fox."

Ages 13 and Up

Teenagers are fascinated by death. Serial killers, vengeful ghosts, and bloodthirsty vampires are avidly relished with a fascination that many parents find disturbing. Don't worry, Mom and Dad, it's natural . . . a natural high, that is. When the brain is stimulated by fear, it responds by producing endorphins, the "feel good" chemicals of the body. Audience members who giggle at tense parts of your story are giving you a compliment – they were *so* scared that their automatic fear system kicked in, making them laugh nervously. And who hasn't screamed with delight on a roller coaster? Teens, especially, love that natural endorphin high that safe fears incite.

Tell teenagers your most blood-curdling, hair-raising PG-13 urban legends. They'll love you for it. Unhappy endings are expected, and the dangers may be as realistic as the gory descriptions. I offer two cautions, however: 1) Violence only, no sex. Parents will accept gruesome bloodshed, but they'll raise the roof if you mention a woman's bare breasts! 2) Use only mild swearing, if any, and only if appropriate to the story. Swear words carry a shock value that can be distracting. Favorite urban legends are "Bloody Mary," "Murderer under the Bed," or "The Babysitter." Stories by Edgar Allan Poe or H. P. Lovecraft, and intense versions of "La Llorona," "Mr. Fox," or "Skeleton Woman" are perfect.

Tips for an Enjoyable Show

For audiences with wide age ranges, tell them you'll start with stories suitable for younger kids, but promise the last story will be *really* scary. Announce when you're at the last story and give more fearful children a chance to leave. Older kids can enjoy the tamer stories knowing that they'll get a treat at the end. Parents appreciate this courtesy and still feel they got their money's worth.

Use "Movie Ratings" guidelines. I identify my stories as *G, PG,* etc. In this way parents can determine in advance if the event is appropriate for their children.

Calm Frightened Children

- Sympathize and apologize: "Yeah, that last one was scary. I'm sorry."
- Never tease or make kids feel bad about their fear.
- Offer reassurances such as, "That could *never* happen here," "Nothing bad will happen to you," or, "That was far away and long ago, there's nothing to worry about." Don't say, "It's just a story." Remember, young children can't distinguish between fantasy and reality, so to them it's very real.

You will frighten children with ghost stories, but they will be frightened in a healthy, happy, positive way. Kids and parents will love you for it!

Resources

Cantor, Joanne. *Mommy, I'm Scared: How TV and Movies Frighten Children and What We Can Do to Protect Them.* Orlando, Florida: Harcourt, Brace & Company, 1998.

Dozier, Rush W., Jr. *Fear Itself, The Origin and Nature of the Powerful Emotion That Shapes Our Lives and Our World.* NY: St. Martin's Griffin, 1998

Dziemianowicz, Stefan. *Bloody Mary and Other Tales for a Dark Night.* NY: Barnes & Noble Books, 2000. Terrific PG-13 tales and legends.

Jones, Gerard. *Killing Monsters: Why Children Need Fantasy, Super Heroes, and Make-Believe Violence.* NY: Basic Books, 2002.

Olson, Arielle North and Howard Schwartz. *Ask the Bones.* NY: Viking, 1999. Delightfully re-written folktales from around the world, great for G through PG.

Repchuk, Caroline. *Classic Spooky Stories.* Bath, UK: Dempsey Parr, an imprint of Parragon, 1999. Ideal G-rated stories

Schwartz, Alvin. *Scary Stories to Tell in the Dark* series. NY: HarperCollins, 1981. Great "bare bones" PG and PG-13 stories to inspire your own versions.

Young, Richard and Judy Dockrey. *Favorite Scary Stories of American Children.* Little Rock, AR: August House, 1999. Includes recommended ratings, G through PG.

Diane Ladley *of Aurora, IL, tells ghost stories – and only ghost stories! Named "America's Ghost Storyteller," Diane's performances of tales, songs, and poems, ranging from G- to X-rated, shiver spines and tickle funny bones. Her tale, "The Liver," won a 2003 Storytelling World Honor award. www.ghoststories.biz*

Participation in Stories

by Joey Talbert

Audience participation gives listeners an active role in storytelling, as they use their voices and bodies to add to the story itself. Participation may take many forms: repeating phrases, songs, chants, movements, or sound effects; answering direct questions, or joining in with call and response. A storyteller can teach the participation before starting the story, or stop the story to encourage it, or merely indicate that the audience should join in during the tale.

Repeated phrases are present in many folktales. "Rumpelstiltskin," "The Three Little Pigs," "Goldilocks and the Three Bears," "The Three Billy Goats Gruff," "Jack and the Beanstalk," and many others contain refrains that are perfect for encouraging audience participation. When choosing phrases for audience members to say with you, make sure they are repeated at least three times in the story. Add recurrent movements or facial expressions to reinforce the repeated lines.

The first time that the storyteller introduces a refrain, the audience listens to the teller's words and tone. For example, in "The Three Billy Goats Gruff," the teller might introduce the troll by scowling, putting her hands on her hips, and in a low voice growling, "Who's that tripping over my bridge?" The second time, the line is familiar to the audience. By the third time, the listeners will anticipate the words and, with a little encouragement, look forward to joining in.

Storytellers may also make up chants to go with a repeating portion of a story. For "Rumpelstiltskin" you might say, "I can spin straw into gold / To save the miller's daughter from the lies her father told," while spinning your hands. Say it first during the course of the story, then stop and explain to the audience that they can help you as the rhyme repeats. Practice it with them slowly while doing the hand motions. For young audiences, break it down and teach it one line at a time. When it comes up again, move your hands and nod to indicate that the audience should begin, and say it with them. By the next time, the listeners should come in on their own when you spin your hands. Pause to give them time to pick up the cue, and always be ready to say it with them if need be. Participation should be enjoyable to the listeners and not feel like a test.

Stories in which a character sings are perfect for encouraging children to join in. In "The Gunniwolf," a little girl saves herself from the wolf with her favorite song. Children enjoy helping the girl get away by singing louder and louder. If a story does not include a song, create one using a familiar tune. Children will be much more likely to join in if they know the melody. In "Henny Penny," for example, the animals could sing to the tune of "Scotland's Burning": "Sky is falling, sky is falling. Follow me, follow me. Run! Run! Run! Run! Tell the king, tell the king!"

Movements and sound effects can be incorporated into almost any story. If a character shakes his head, claps his hands, or rolls his eyes, encourage the children to do so too. If the wind blows, the dog barks, or the gate squeaks, give the audience time to create the sounds with you. Participation is most effective when it pairs sound and movement together. But beware of making the telling overly complicated; participation should add to the story without distracting from the plot.

With some stories, you can divide listeners into groups and have each group make a different sound effect. In "The Fisherman and His Wife," I split my audience of elementary school students into wind, ocean, and seagulls. Each time the fisherman calls the fish, the audience creates these sounds of the sea, increasing the volume and intensity as the fish becomes more agitated.

Pre-schoolers appreciate the use of questions. Developmentally, they are in the egocentric phase – the world revolves around them. Therefore, they need the story to relate directly to them, and answering questions fills this need. Ask questions to which you have already supplied the answer. For example, in "The Three Little Pigs," you might pause after the pigs have built their houses to ask, "The wolf knocked on the door of the first house which was made of . . . what?" Reply to answers in a positive fashion even if the response is incorrect. Direct questions with concrete answers help the children to review and retain the thread of the story. They are especially useful when young minds wander.

Call and response is a very stylized type of participation. Some Native American tellers call "Ho!" and the audience answers, "Hey!" Expressions may be specific to a story, culture, or even the storyteller himself. Rhode Island teller Len Cabral tells a story about why the sky is so high. He asks, "Wha?" and the audience responds, "'sup." Plan each time you will do a call and response so as not to disturb the rhythm of the tale. As you get comfortable with this technique, you will be able to use it whenever you need to shake up the listeners.

Audience participation serves to involve children in a hands-on, enjoyable way, whether with verbal or physical involvement, or both. The story becomes an experience to be discovered together. Plan your participation ahead of time, but be open to following your audience's lead to find that which works best for you, your story, and your listeners.

> ***Joey Talbert*** *is a professional storyteller and a drama instructor. She has led workshops for the Sharing the Fire conference in Boston, MA and the NSN Pre-conference in Denver, CO. Her article on telling to pre-school audiences was published in the July 2002 "Tale Trader." Joeydramaqueen@aol.com*

Six Steps Towards Developing Sound Stories

by Elizabeth Falconer

Whether or not you are an experienced musician, you can use instruments and sound to enhance and transform your stories. I use the word "sound" rather than "music" in order to be free from preconceived ideas of music and all of the "good" and "bad" associations the word may hold.

Sound triggers the imagination, adds depth to your story, and is entertaining for the listener. Adding sound elements helps to provide memory clues as you tell the story and may give you something to do with your hands – in this way, it can even make story preparation easier for the teller. Incorporating sound also fosters a more intimate relationship with the story, because you are forced to analyze it deeply as you prepare it with sound, rather than accept the story passively "as is." This helps to ensure that the telling itself will emanate ease and excitement while reflecting your individual style.

But . . . how to make a "sound story"? Here are six basic guidelines towards developing the kind of story that will reverberate with your listeners:

1) Limit yourself to one instrument per story; it can be anything from a drum to a violin, a guitar to a cymbal. If you are an experienced sound-ician, momentarily set aside everything you usually worry about regarding playing "right." You are about to create something unique to go with your storytelling. Look at the instrument and remember those first feelings you had when you began to play, when anything was possible and you weren't worried about making mistakes. If you are a novice player who just picked up something handy that makes noise, or finally took that untouched guitar out of the closet, then don't worry! As Miles Davis said, "Do not fear mistakes – there are none."

Some instruments, of course, are easier to approach

than others. Visit a percussion shop, a world instrument store, or a good independent children's toy or bookstore for some ideas. (Oh, yes – music stores are an option, too!) Pick instruments up and make sounds – what speaks to you? Close your eyes and listen. Maracas, bells, mbira (thumb pianos), xylophones, ocarinas, flutes and drums work well. If you don't have to tune it yourself and it costs less than twenty dollars it could be very, very useful!

2) Play – literally! – with your instrument. Of course, you know that a hand drum is usually played by hitting it in the middle. But what other sounds can it make? What happens when you rub your hands on it? Tap the edges? Experiment, and take notes on what the sounds remind you of. Ask others. "What does this sound like to you?" Outrageous responses sometimes turn out to be the most useful!

Keep in mind what the sound *suggests* to the mind; tinkling sounds can suggest rain, snow, magic, confusion . . . a wide variety of associations are already established, even with sounds outside of our experience – we have never really heard fairy dust! Think of some sounds from nature, and see if you can make your instrument sound like those sounds. Remember, things and ideas that do not have a sound in real life can still be represented by making a sound on your instrument: A rainbow. A tall tree. Fear.

3) Instrument as prop: Now that you are holding it in your hand, don't put it down! It can become a part of the story. Look at your instrument and write down ten things it looks like, or could look like. A tambourine can be a hat, a bowl or a flying saucer, for example. Then, when you are looking at potential stories, imagine what else it could become. Or perhaps you have a story in mind already and want to add music. You can approach it that way, too . . . just keep your mind open to the visual as well as the auditory aspects.

4) Every time you work on your story, from start to finish, keep your instrument in your lap or close by, and refer to it often. You may find that just making a few sounds as you say sentences out loud will lead to new ideas. And those ideas will lead to more new ideas . . .

5) Analyze your story and break it down into characters and scenes. For example, if there are four main characters such as three bears and a little girl, find a sound to associate with each character, and repeat it each time that character appears. It can be as simple as changing a drumbeat: strong and slow for Papa Bear, faster for Mama and then Baby, an erratic beat for Goldilocks. Do the same for places and/or scenes in the story. Experiment broadly and then keep what works best for you.

6) As with all storytelling and music-making, don't forget to practice! Practice using your instrument and telling your story – deciding exactly how you will hold the instrument, when you will sit or stand, and when you will play – until the sound becomes an integral part of the tale.

Simple instrumental sounds can engage listeners on a deep level. Children's imaginations are especially activated by sounds. And your own storytelling approach and appreciation can be broadened with this experience. By incorporating some kind of instrumental sound into your telling, you will be further connected to the story and the telling. Instrument in hand, tiptoe with excitement into a story. And watch out . . . you just may find yourself becoming a sound storyteller!

> *Elizabeth Falconer* *came to storytelling as a composer and master of the Japanese koto, a 13-string classical instrument. Her unique recordings of Japanese folktales with koto accompaniment have brought her national awards. Further information on her activities and award-winning Koto World label can be found at her website, www.kotoworld.com.*

Using Puppets to Tell Stories

by Susanna "Granny Sue" Holstein

Puppets are visually attractive; they give color, texture, and dimension to a story. Puppets provide visual clues to the story's meaning, add dialogue and opportunities for interaction, and can connect the storyteller to hard-to-reach audiences.

Puppets as Storytelling Partners

Children begin to personify inanimate objects at an early age; using puppets in storytelling with children is a natural extension of this interest. Puppets may be used in introductions, as main characters or narrators, or as secondary characters manipulated by the audience.

Batsy Bybell of Idaho uses her parrot puppet "Tooter Two" to introduce her performances. Tooter Two pulls Bybell's hair, bites her ears, and generally misbehaves, to the delight of the audience. The puppet's outrageous behavior creates a laughing community of listeners.

A puppet might be the main character or narrator of a story. The storyteller can add dialogue between himself and the puppet to heighten audience interest and add another voice. For example, consider this exchange:

Storyteller: Why did you kiss the princess, Mr. Frog?

Puppet: Because I'm a prince, remember?

Storyteller: Well, I bet she didn't like being kissed by your slimy lips!

Frog: Oh yeah, how do you know? You've never kissed me! Wanna give it a try?

A puppet can act out parts of a story, with the storyteller as narrator. The puppet provides action and perhaps a few lines of dialogue. One of my favorite stories told in this way features a raccoon puppet. I tell the story to both the audience and the puppet. The puppet only speaks a few lines himself. He increases interest in the story through his actions, providing a different perspective for listeners.

A storyteller may invite selected audience members to operate puppets. When telling the traditional story of "The Little Red Hen" I manipulate the hen puppet myself, and invite children to join in the story by choosing a puppet from my supply. I do not limit them to barnyard animals, so the story becomes a creative process in which the children have individual input.

Selecting a Story

Not all stories are suitable for telling with a puppet. A good story candidate will have one main character and few secondary characters. Poems, songs, and stories with simple plots, chants, or repeated lines are all possible puppet stories.

Puppet stories should be short. It can be difficult to maintain the puppet's voice for long periods. Fables are excellent puppet stories: they are brief, have one or two characters, and easily invite repetition, chants, and other modes of audience participation.

Selecting a Puppet

Choose puppets with appealing characteristics. A storytelling puppet must be large enough to be seen by your entire audience. Be sure the puppet's eyes are large and visible. Storytellers rely on eye contact to connect with audiences, and puppets need that same connection to be successful.

Finding a puppet's personality is a voyage of discovery. It requires working with the puppet, exploring its movement options, and testing its audience appeal. My raccoon puppet, for instance, has a specific voice and is generally grouchy in the mornings. I discovered these traits through using the puppet in the telling of "his" story.

Some of my puppets never get names or develop personalities. Perhaps someday I will find just the right story and personality for each of them. Still, they are very useful as stock characters that can be used in a variety of stories.

Puppet and Audience Management

Your puppet's voice must be loud enough to be heard by your audience, clear enough to be understood, and consistent throughout. Remember, you will have to maintain the voice you choose throughout the story. Experiment with voices to find the right one. Accents add interest, but use them only if you can sustain them and the audience can understand them.

The puppet must be easy to manipulate. It is important to remember the puppet's body structure. Where is the puppet's neck? Back? Waist? Movements must be realistic and believable. Practice in front of a mirror to be sure the puppet's movements are natural and comfortable. *Making Puppets Come Alive* by Larry Engler provides photos and exercises for a wide variety of puppet movements.

A puppet dangling and ignored on the teller's hand will destroy the illusion of the puppet as a live participant. When it is inactive, make a "floor" for the puppet with the opposite arm, hold it on your lap, or move the puppet behind your back.

Plan how you will store your puppets before and during your performance. I use a wheeled suitcase for easy transportation. Plastic totes, boxes, and tote bags are other options. Consider how you will carry your items into the performance area.

Displays of puppets can provide an interesting backdrop to your performance. Check ahead of time to be sure a table is available or bring a lightweight folding table with you. I use filled water bottles for stands; the bottles provide a rounded, natural shape for the puppets' bodies. Inexpensive paper towel holders and rolled magazines can also be used to hold puppets erect. But if you are performing for very young children who might be distracted by a puppet display, consider keeping the puppets out of sight until they are needed.

Set simple, understandable rules before inviting audience members to use the puppets. For example: puppets do not fight or bite; when the story is over, puppets must go back on the table so that other puppets can tell stories; always take your puppet off gently. At the conclusion of the story, thank each child and ask for applause. This offers reinforcement for the children and provides an opportunity to gather the puppets and prepare for the next story.

Planning and practice are the keys to successful storytelling with puppets. Purchase, gather, or construct your materials, think through how you will handle your puppets, and practice each story with the puppets to be used. You will add an exciting new dimension to your storytelling which appeals to audiences of all learning styles and abilities.

Resources

Champline, Connie, and Nancy Renfro. *Storytelling with Puppets*. Chicago: ALA, 1997.

Engler, Larry. *Making Puppets Come Alive*. NY: Dover, 1997.

Van Schuyver, Jan. *Storytelling Made Easy with Puppets*. Phoenix, AZ: Oryx Press, 1993.

Granny Sue is the National Storytelling Network Liaison for West Virginia. When she's not telling stories, she is Branch Services Manager for the Kanawha County Public Library System. Granny Sue lives in Jackson County, West Virginia. holstein_susanna@hotmail.com

Let Your Story Move You: Authentic Movement in Storytelling

by Jackson Gillman

Storytelling is visual – whether or not the listener is actually seeing the teller. At its best, a well-told story evokes a series of images – the listeners "see" the story as it is told. Many things go into creating this magic. Some stories need only the spoken or written word. Others can be told wordlessly via illustration, mime, dance, or music. Just as stories can take a variety of forms, so too do listeners have a variety of listening styles. Some are easily engaged by words alone. Others benefit from the assistance of melody or rhythm. And many benefit from seeing the action of the story portrayed.

There are some pieces in my repertoire for which I'll use as much stage area as I possibly can. For others, I will simply sit and tell. The story itself informs my choice of movement. A quiet, reflective tale may call for economical gestures, while a story with lots of action and "over the top" characters benefits from more movement. My advice: don't try to find ways to make your stories move, let the stories move you.

When a story attracts me enough to want to tell it, I "see" it in my mind's eye. As I rehearse, my visualization of the setting and action becomes clearer and more detailed. I try to "place" imaginary objects and scenes in the space and to be consistent in where they are. I develop identifying traits for the characters, physical as well as vocal, and visualize their relationships to each other and to the audience.

When a story is from personal experience, we have little trouble envisioning the setting. We know where, what, and how things happened, so it is easy to find ways to authentically move about in the imagined space. A good way to start the process of concretizing a story's setting is to actually move, making distances, positions, and activities as real as possible. From this exercise, it becomes easier to convey setting and action on a smaller scale.

I remember being swept up by the performance of an amateur teller at a story swap. A burly, retired Boston Police officer told about the time he was put on mounted patrol and the fiasco that resulted because he had absolutely no control of his horse. He moved around throughout his telling with surprising grace. He didn't need any mime training to appear to be riding a horse. He was seeing and remembering that wild ride – he was *on* that horse. And I was right with him every *clop* of the way.

Whenever possible: show, don't tell. Use your face to show emotion rather than describing or telling about an emotion. Use your body to indicate tension or fright rather than declaring, "He was tense," or "She was scared."

Be *in* the setting. Change your focus to see the events in front of you, and react to the sight. This assists listeners in imagining the scene. It's okay to not look at the audience. In fact, at times it's better to remain in the story, "seeing" what the narrator or characters are seeing. But don't lose sight of your audience. Be aware of what you are showing them. Experiment so that peak moments have the greatest impact.

Once you feel comfortable with your work, find a friend or colleague to give you feedback. An outside eye is always a good idea. The listener can help identify the effectiveness of your movements as well as other aspects of the story.

When tellers don't have a clear or consistent picture in their own mind, movements may be vague. The story may seem to change point of view. Perhaps it is unclear when the teller is speaking as the narrator, when as a character. As a visual listener, I find that this lack of spatial clarity has a disorienting effect on me; I flounder about trying to get my bearings. There are those in your audience, myself included, who best "see" the story when the teller has made an effort to clearly "landscape" it.

Be aware that too much movement can also distract the listeners – more can easily end up being less. For example, when switching from one character to another, there's no need to jump from one side to the other. A signature attitude, a simple tilt of the head, or an adjustment of eye focus may be enough to differentiate characters. Find ways to move about as efficiently as possible.

Although the late, beloved Jackie Torrence stayed seated when she told stories, she certainly moved, and moved very well. With her facial expressions – particularly her use of her eyes – and gestures, she simply and articulately illustrated the story's pictures. Nothing more was needed.

Something magical happens when tellers have a clear vision of the action in a story. They are consistent with the characters and their relationships, with the placement of imaginary props and whole landscapes. If they really see it happening, tellers can use detailed, naturalistic movements which enable the listeners to clearly experience the characters, emotions, and settings in the story.

So, in a nutshell: visualize your stories' actions clearly, refine those images, rehearse moving about in your settings as comfortably as you're able, then get out there, relax, and let the story move you.

> *Jackson Gillman*'s background in mime, dance, and sign language is clearly evident in his performances and in his "Storyscaping" coaching. "Gillman is a masterly storyteller, carving entire street scenes with single gestures. His only prop is the space, which he uses with a painter's appreciation for visual composition." –Christian Science Monitor www.jacksongillman.com

Rediscovering Childhood Tales – for Every Age

by Marni Gillard

When I first stumbled into the art of storytelling, I forgot that I carried stories deep inside, tales that had touched me when I was very young. Dutifully I combed the library's 398.2 shelves for fairy tales or the children's section for picture books, looking for stories to tell. But when I rediscovered an old collection that my mother had read to me when I was a child, I shivered as I looked through its pages. I knew I had found a whole new repertoire. And, I realized, *The Road in Story Land* wasn't just for the young. It resonated with listeners of all ages.

The Pine Tree and Its Needles

In this tale, a pine tree is unhappy with its prickly needles. It wishes aloud for gold leaves that will sparkle in the sunlight. A kindhearted fairy obliges, turning the needles into coins. The birds, bees, and sun admire the coins, but that night a robber steals them. Next, the tree wishes for glass leaves (which the wind breaks) and then oak leaves (which a billy goat eats). It isn't truly happy until it has its needles back again.

When I first saw the picture of the robber stealing the tree's coins, and then saw the glass leaves, my heart beat faster. This pine tree was me!

As a child, I spoke all the character voices while my mother narrated the story. I especially loved the fairy's sing-song, "Little pine tree, little pine tree, you shall have your wish!" Had my mother understood how I dreamed of splendid clothes instead of hand-me-downs? Had she known I wished for a wise big sister instead of pesky little ones? Since I associated the story with my early childhood, I first told it only to young children. Then a fifth-grade teacher requested I tell it to her class.

"Oh, no," I laughed. "It's so childish."

"Well, *I* like it," she countered. "Grow it up!"

Although my childhood yearnings had been replaced by adult desires, I still longed to be different and somehow better. So the pine tree still lived within me; the themes still resonated. The fairy became a spirit. The pine tree matured into a pre-teen. I deepened my voice and omitted the audience participation. The teacher grinned as she and the fifth-graders joined me deep in the woods. The tale successfully "grew up."

The Greedy Old Woman and Her Cakes

An old woman in a black dress, white apron, and red scarf refuses to share her plump cakes with a passing stranger. As a child, I knew I was like her. I hated giving up the biggest cookie or sharing my favorite toys. As my mother read the tale, I imagined I rolled and patted and smelled the sweet dough just as the old woman did. The woman tries to make a tiny cake to give to a stranger, but each little cake magically grows bigger. She can't give away such a big cake. I understood!

When the stranger turned away, I would feel scared. I knew that whatever magic had changed those cakes would change the old woman, too. For her stinginess, she is turned into a bird. When, on the final page, my mother read, "Now she'll have to peck, peck, peck, just to find a fat beetle or bug," I would cringe and vow never to be selfish again.

This *pourquoi* tale points to the greed we get stuck in throughout our lives. And it helps us poke fun at ourselves. When I tell the story, I slowly shrink from woman to bird, feeling my nose sharpen and my arms turn to wings. Some listeners shiver and some grin. Then, as my mother did with me, I help listeners return to their world, saying: "You might see that old woman in a tree today. You'll hear her peck-pecking away. Look for her black and white feathers and red-feathered head." I continue slowly, so the listeners can find their voices. "Remember . . . " I say. "Remember, she was turned into a —." And in that pause, we dare to say "woodpecker." Children shout. Adults often whisper. No matter our age, the story's magic and wisdom speaks to us.

Finding the Stories in You

What stories live in you, waiting to be told? Not every tale from childhood still resonates with me, but I do remember favorite characters, images, and refrains. I see Midas turning his daughter to gold. I hear the troll holler, "Who's that trip-trapping across my bridge?" When I tell any tale, I listen once again. Each story lets me know how to tell it. The faces in each audience show me how to "grow it up" or package it "pint-sized."

Many of us carry stories with themes similar to those in *The Road in Storyland*. The universal themes of greed and generosity, innocence, and transformation call to listeners of every age. Deeply ingrained feelings from childhood and our own adult yearnings may lead us back to such tales. What bits of story do you still hear? What images can you still see? Perhaps, like the tales I re-discovered, your childhood favorites still speak to you. Have fun finding the stories once planted in you. Open your mouth, let them out!

References

Piper, Watty, ed. [1932] 1952. "The Pine Tree and Its Needles" and "The Old Woman Who Wanted All the Cakes," *The Road in Storyland*. NY: Platt & Munk, (out of print).

*Marni Gillard is the author of **Storyteller, Storyteacher: The Power of Storytelling for Teaching and Living** (Portland, ME: Sternhouse, 1996). She recorded five life tales on **Without a Splash: Diving into Childhood Memories**. At The Story Studio in Schenectady, New York, Marni offers classes about finding the stories within. www.marnigillard.com*

A Moving Target –
Telling at Fairs and Festivals

by Batsy Bybell

Sooner or later it happens to all tellers: the request to tell stories at a mall, fair, or festival. Since we don't want to turn down an engagement, we agree to participate. But inwardly, the worries start niggling – how can we possibly succeed at a venue like this?

Telling stories to a mobile audience requires a shift inside the teller's mind. Normal expectations of what constitutes a good performance go out the window. Instead of a quiet, focused group in an enclosed space, there may be constant interruptions, poor acoustics, and less than perfect visibility. But there are ways to turn these headaches into assets. Once I became open to the possibilities facing me, challenges grew into opportunities. I decided to abandon my preconceptions and experiment by walking around while telling stories. I became a roving performer, and I love it.

A Necessary Hook

An attention grabber is essential to be noticed and lure the audience closer. I first establish eye contact with possible listeners. As with improvisational street theater, I must enter the audience's space and be immediately entertaining. I use a hook to slow the pace of someone walking by and help create an initial reaction. Hooks may be colorful costumes, intriguing props, irresistible one-liners, large puppets, or a combination of these – whatever works for you.

For example, if I'm dressed as a pirate I call out, "Hey, Matey! Care to join me on a treasure hunt?" Once a listener stops, I hand her a map marked with simple clues. I explain how to follow the clues to buried treasure (a pot of wrapped candy watched over by a colleague) while telling a short story of how parrots learned to talk. Other listeners stop, and I've got my audience.

Sometimes I use puppets or props to immediately draw attention. My parrot puppet squawks and nibbles on shiny jewelry or tries to steal food from potential listeners. My witch puppet asks flirtatiously, "Have you tried this new wrinkle cream? Use it and look like me." On a blustery day, a small dragon puppet nestles inside my cape, unsuccessfully spouting flames. Other times I am costumed as a Story Weaver carrying a basket filled with small figures, each one connected to a tale. I hawk my wares like a street vendor, "Come hear a story spun for you – bold knights and fearsome dragons, true love and ugly trolls."

Once I've caught the attention of listeners, I tell short, lively stories lasting no more than two to five minutes. This is not the time for a long, complex tale filled with descriptive details. Brief fables and *pourquoi* (how and why) stories are perfect for this type of telling. Tie the stories to the hook, the event, or a giveaway item.

Attitude is Everything

To tell successfully in a busy venue requires total commitment to being outgoing, outrageous, and animated. The teller has been hired as entertainment, which means he needs to enter 100% into the spirit of the occasion. I wander freely around. I stand in aisles and entertain people waiting in line for food or rides. I ask ancient riddles as I stroll through a Renaissance Fair.

These events generally draw audiences of all ages. Remember to tell to whoever is standing in front of you, whatever their age. It helps to be glib enough to improvise freely and banter with one and all. After telling a quick story, I move on to the next target audience. That way, if no one stops, I know the next listener is just a few steps further. It's hard to not feel personally offended when everyone seems to rush by. But maybe they have another commitment – or even a pressing need for the bathroom.

Roving telling is also the perfect opportunity to pass out memory anchors. Any small giveaway that listeners can take home delights them and reminds them of you and your stories. I pass out little bears when I tell "Why the Bear has a Stumpy Tail." A bookmark, a picture . . . if your name and contact information are visible, what better way to incorporate marketing? You'll be promoting your storytelling and remembered for future occasions.

Tips for the Teller

I design special costumes or wear distinctive clothes, with comfort and ease of movement in mind. Tugging down a garment or holding onto a hat in windy weather would distract me from my audience. If the site is outdoors, I prepare for all types of weather and dress in layers. I wear comfortable walking shoes and incorporate pockets into all of my outfits. I always carry business cards, brochures, and water along with promotional handouts. Some roving performers carry a bag or basket for these. Because audiences are close, I don't need amplification. I pre-arrange a location on-site in which to stash my surplus supplies and props.

This type of performance can be very demanding because you are "on" the entire time. I try to schedule fifteen-minute breaks every hour or two. But it is also supremely satisfying because of the high level of personal interaction with all audience members. The next time you're asked to tell at a fair or mall, be open to inspiration. Play with improvisation. Try something different and see if it works for you.

> *Batsy Bybell is a professional storyteller-puppeteer and Outreach Services Librarian in northern Idaho. She has been a featured performer at the Stories by the Sea and Northlands festivals, and across the Pacific Northwest. Puppets and "walkarounds" became her playful way to introduce storytelling to a wider audience. www.storyteller.net/tellers/batsy*

Children with Special Needs

by Gwyn Calvetti

Telling stories to children with special needs presents special challenges. Meeting these challenges will bring joy to them while helping us grow as tellers. I've told stories to children with a wide variety of disabilities, and each child teaches me something new about storytelling. Every disability is unique and presents different opportunities and considerations. The key, as with any storytelling event, is finding that teller-listener connection that brings the magic into the tale.

Storytellers are likely to encounter special needs children anywhere kids gather. "Full inclusion" describes the educational shift from separating children in special education classes to including them in the mainstream with their peers. As a result, kids with disabilities are taking part in schools, scout troops, or summer camps along with their able-bodied counterparts. They may have cognitive or emotional disabilities, hearing impairment, autism spectrum disorders, cerebral palsy, or a bewildering array of syndromes and medical conditions.

Effective pre-show planning can avoid many problems. Ask your contact person about any children who may have special needs, and what behavior you may expect from them. If you are not familiar with the characteristics of a particular disability, spend time researching it. Find out if the children will be accompanied by an adult. Many younger children in schools have an "inclusion aide" who travels with them throughout the day.

Ask if listeners use adaptive equipment, such as an FM amplification system sometimes used for hearing-impaired children. If so, arrange to arrive early and familiarize yourself with its use, so that you will be at ease and can direct your energy toward the children and your stories.

If possible, request that audiences be small in size. Children with special needs may have difficulty maintaining attention. A small group limits distractions and allows you to use proximity to help listeners focus and connect with the story. You may want to suggest a shorter program length for these groups as well, since the children may fatigue easily or attend for shorter times than their peers.

Location can hinder or enhance the experience. Many special needs children are very sensitive to loud noises and large spaces. A small, carpeted performance area will make the children feel more comfortable and able to focus.

Many children with hearing impairments or on the autism spectrum are strong visual learners. Make use of props, musical instruments, or movement and strong facial expressions. These children often respond well to rhythm and music, as well.

Story length and complexity should match the developmental age of the mainstream if your setting is one with full inclusion. If you are telling for a group that involves special needs children only, ask your contact person what would be appropriate for them developmentally and match your stories to that level. Stories that involve the listeners physically or verbally will also engage these children better than more reflective tales.

During performances, I've learned to expect the unexpected and to be flexible when it occurs. I've had children call out inappropriate remarks, repeat refrains long after the story has continued on, or even make such loud noises, without any obvious provocation, that the teacher has removed them from the room.

At the beginning of the performance, be in place, waiting for the children to arrive. Give everyone a few minutes to settle in, look you over, and make comments before you begin your program. Often, kids with special needs lack age-appropriate social skills, and may blurt out remarks about your appearance, your props, or anything that has caught their attention. This isn't meant to offend, so listen, respond with a smile, and go on.

Don't be surprised if they call out indiscriminately or repeat a line that strikes them. Acknowledge their behavior – with a nod or a comment or an improvised remark – and move your story along, perhaps adding a new twist to an old favorite to incorporate what you hear. Some special needs children have disorders in timing; they repeat things too much, laugh too late or too loudly, or clap out of turn.

The responsible adult may choose to remove the student if he becomes disruptive. This can be unsettling; realize that it isn't a reflection on your performance, but a way to help the child pull himself together to enjoy the program or keep him from distracting others.

Make an effort to approach your listeners during your program, but be aware that their idea of personal space may be different from what you expected. Moving into their space and line of vision will increase the chances that they engage with your story. They may not be able to make the kind of eye contact you expect due to physical disabilities or interpersonal issues, but that doesn't mean they aren't with you.

If a story involves members of the audience, try to include at least one of these "special" children, even if it's simply to hold a prop for you. The other children in their class often become actively involved in helping them and take a great deal of pride in seeing them succeed.

Most of all, enjoy telling stories to all kinds of children, knowing you are giving them the gift of your time and talent. In return, they may gift you with new insights for your next program!

Gwyn Calvetti has worked as a speech/language pathologist in the schools for over twenty years. Her students enjoy her storytelling daily, as she spins tales to meet their educational goals. Gwyn lives in southwestern Wisconsin and is a member of several storytelling organizations, including Northlands Storytelling Network. rcalvettijr@centurytel.net

Distractions: Take Charge, Incorporate, or Surrender!

by Cindy Killavey

The wandering toddler in the third row, the parents in the back chatting away, the sudden boom of thunder that shakes the room. Distractions can come in any size, shape, or sound. But how do you deal with them?

First and foremost, clearly communicate with your host what you require. Discuss how the audience will be sitting, the space, the light, the sound, your needs, and the needs of the audience. When performing outdoors, ask about a back-up plan for stormy weather. (Don't accept "it never rains.") In any situation, find out what else is happening in the area. Is there a loud Country Western band nearby? Will bells ring in the middle of your scheduled performance? Is the library next to the fire station? Educate your employer about what works best for you. Then: be prepared to take charge, adjust, incorporate, and improvise.

Give yourself the gift of time. Arrive early enough to inspect the performance space, introduce yourself to the host and janitor, then make any needed changes prior to audience arrival.

Where are the restrooms and entrances and exits? It is very distracting to have audience members passing behind you during a show. Try to position your back against a solid, windowless wall, with exits or restrooms at the far end of the space.

Can the audience see and hear you clearly? Can you see them? Can lights be turned on, adjusted, or set up for you? *Buzz, buzz, click, click, whirr.* Listen for clanking heaters, loud air conditioning, humming fluorescent lights, music or announcements. Ask for the host or janitor's assistance.

The unexpected does happen. As a beginning storyteller I once got lost and arrived "in the nick of time" for a performance at an elementary school. I had not arranged the seating ahead of time. The children marched into the gymnasium and proceeded to sit in a wide circle around me. We were going to do "theater in the round!" It was immediately obvious to me that this was not going to work. I rearranged the audience so they were all sitting in front of me auditorium style, then went forward.

Eshu Bumpus, a wonderful storyteller from Massachusetts, says that in schools, sooner or later you will have to deal with someone in the audience getting sick during a performance. This is an obvious showstopper. Clean-up can't wait. Eshu used this opportunity to chat with the audience about being kind to the boy who got sick – and to the boy sitting in front of him who needed a change of clothes.

Sounds from outside the room may interrupt your stories. Sirens, train whistles, or thunder can be acknowledged and addressed without breaking the flow of your performance. I have added "a clap of thunder shook the room" or "the wind howled" to a story while a storm raged outside. Ed Stivender, a consummate storyteller, once abandoned the tale he was telling and launched into a story on trains when the sounds of a nearby train wouldn't stop. The audience appreciated his quick thinking.

Family shows should be delightful occasions with adults and children enjoying stories together. Unfortunately, many parents think of storytelling as "just for the kiddies" and want to gather at the back and chat. Or they decide that their six-month-old would *love* to hear stories and then don't seem to know what to do when the baby starts fussing or her older sibling insists on talking. Then, of course, there is that "wandering toddler."

Alert your host that parents and children should sit together. Invite them again yourself if necessary. During interactive stories I remind parents to "set the example." Sometimes I give the adults a specific role. In "The Bremen Town Musicians," for example, I divide the audience into groups to make the animal chorus and I end with "all the grown-ups can be the donkey with me." If adult chatter still gets disruptive, it often works to pause and look questioningly toward the source of the noise.

Assure audience members at the beginning of the show that it is okay to leave with a fussing baby or a talkative child. Arrange with the host to remind parents to go outside if necessary. When one young audience member kept talking, storyteller Judith Black asked if he wanted to tell his own story later. Another tack might be to simply say, "it's *my* turn to talk now."

Sometimes young children wander onto the stage, reaching for instruments or props, or just taking focus from the teller. Storyteller Carolyn Martino dealt with a wee one at her feet by asking, "Who belongs to this child?" Another teller took the hand of a toddling child and gently led her back to the woman who was obviously her mother, while still narrating the tale.

Distractions are out there, like gremlins lurking in the forest, waiting to upset you, throw you off balance, and ruin your performance. Don't let them. Try to anticipate and plan for all you can. Then, take a deep breath and accept the situation, and do your best with humor, grace, and a positive, flexible attitude. Armed with knowledge and your own successful experiences, go forth to win the day and live happily ever after.

> *Cindy Killavey* is an award-winning storyteller who has performed throughout the Northeast. She is a Rhode Island Folk Arts/Education roster artist. Cindy helped found and produces the Rhode Island Storytelling Festival. She recently published *The Stories We Tell*, a collection of stories, songs, and poems by Rhode Island Storytellers. www.storyri.com

Cultural Sensitivity: A Bridge for Communication

by Judith Black

You can't take people anywhere unless you begin the journey where they are. Cultural sensitivity is about this place of embarkation, and the journey into the listeners' world or into uncharted waters. Saul Alinsky, one of the greatest community organizers of the past century, always told his minions, "Don't bring a ham and cheese sandwich to a meeting at the Jewish Community Center." If you begin an interaction by offending a group's cultural sensibilities, chances are they won't travel anywhere with you in the driver's seat.

Translation: when telling stories to children, first offer mirrors of their lives before taking them through windows. The mirrors are the parts of stories in which they see themselves reflected. The windows are invitations into possibility.

Begin with Mirrors

Stories that have an ethnic, social, emotional, physical, or cognitive resonance with listeners establish a bridge of cultural understanding. In order to effect this you need to know who your listeners are. Get information that will enable you to make culturally sensitive choices. For instance, you might not want to start a program in an Armenian community with a Turkish folktale, given the history of the two countries. (You might end with it, but only if you are sure the listeners are prepared for the journey.)

I was once hired to share stories on the subject of rice with third graders in Lowell, MA. These students, mostly from Cambodia, came from a culture where the smell of rice first touched their senses early in the morning and lingered to kiss them good night as they fell asleep. Their parents were from an agrarian, Buddhist, Pol Pot-shocked culture based on rice. In order to draw these students' hearts and minds into the world of story, I had to immerse myself in their world. Ultimately, this led me to learn that stories from Cambodia have a very different shape and sensibility from ours. I also learned the Khmer words (and pronunciation) for rice grinder, and enjoyed spotting a young face lit up in recognition when I used them.

More Mirrors

Be open to possibilities. Imagine you are sharing a familiar folktale and the heroine is meeting the man of her dreams. You look into the sea of faces living this story with you. Perhaps those faces, unlike the characters in the tale, are Asian, African-American, or Hispanic. The race of your handsome hero suddenly changes. You didn't plan it that way. You've never told it that way before, but looking out you want the listeners to see a hero whom they recognize.

Windows to the World

When we tell stories to draw listeners into specific cultures, we have a responsibility to the tales' origins. I once heard a brilliant teller share a story about a little Jewish "stetl." After the show, I gently shared that the word was pronounced "shtetl." The next time he told the story he said "small Jewish village." What a shame to lose the flavor of language because of insecurity with pronunciation! Many tellers teach about a variety of world cultures through story. But if the tale is not from your own culture, it is incumbent upon you to understand the tale within its context. Learn about its events, images, sounds, and characters. Once you understand them, you are better able to communicate the story (and pronounce the words correctly).

There is one caveat to this. Many members of our first nations have asked contemporary storytellers not to tell their sacred tales. The native cultures of the Americas are numerous and unique. Some tellers have studied with elders and story keepers and have been honored with their stories. If you are not among these, then it is best to share only the lighter tales (such as trickster stories) which have emerged from "the people." I hear this request from many Native Americans; it is worth respecting.

Religion

In today's America, the separation of church and state is becoming less and less defined. In a democracy, part of the responsibility of the state is education, and yet, schools are continually pressed to respond to the theological teachings of specific religious groups among their populations.

Jehovah's Witnesses will not allow their children to listen to stories of ghosts and goblins. Fundamentalist Christians want the biblical story of creation taught instead of the "theory" of evolution. Assembly of God members worked to ban storyteller Nancy Duncan because she portrays the ancient Russian folkloric witch, Baba Yaga. They convinced principals that she was advocating witchcraft, the occult and cannibalism! (Baba Yaga eats the "bad" Russian children.) The list of points of view is endless, and every group claims the high ground. While you are not obliged to represent any given theology within the public schools, you can't ignore the background and belief systems of your audience: you can't take people anywhere unless you begin where they are.

When I am working in Utah, I begin with stories that have a biblical resonance. When working in Nancy Duncan's old stomping ground, I tell stories about traditional family and community values. In each case, I might end with Baba Yaga, or five versions of the creation of earth and its people, but only if I feel that the listeners are ready to travel there with me. Cultural sensitivity is about our ability to understand the world of our listeners, create a mirror for them, and then bring them through the glass to new worlds.

***Judith Black**'s traditional and original works have received standing ovations at the Montreal Comedy Festival, the Smithsonian Institution, the National Storytelling Festival, the Disney Institute and elsewhere. A Massachusetts resident, she has received many awards, including NSN's most prestigious honor, the Oracle Circle of Excellence. www.storiesalive.com*

Storytelling and
State Learning Standards

by Sue Black

The magic and power of storytelling: it's real and it's important. But in this era of "No Child Left Behind," administrators want to know that the storyteller they hire or the storytelling unit in the classroom will result in more than magic. The pressure is on to justify every expenditure and program in terms of student achievement. The focus is narrow and intense: How will *this* improve the test scores?

Storytelling is an important component of a literacy-rich environment; storytellers have the unique opportunity to use their art to contribute to student knowledge and achievement. Each US state has developed its own set of curriculum standards – what each child should learn at each educational level. See your state's Department of Education website to get specific information for each age group and subject. The list below includes many of the language arts and drama learning standards cited by numerous states across the country for grades K-8. Use it in discussions with colleagues or administrators as an affirmation of the importance of storytelling in education, as a base to justify and encourage storytelling programs, or as a way to analyze and assess individual educational attributes of the storytelling art.

Through storytelling, students will:

- Improve listening comprehension and vocabulary
- Listen for the purpose of communicating that information to others

- Improve visualization skills
- Identify patterns and relationships within stories
- Improve awareness of story structure including main idea, sequencing, transitions, beginning, middle, and end
- Identify, compare, contrast, and analyze common themes
- Compare elements of stories from different regions and different times
- Compare and contrast different versions of the same story
- Compare points of view in a variety of works
- Discuss and respond to a variety of literature
- Connect stories with things that happen in their world
- Learn about the relationship between people and their environment
- Make predictions in stories and draw conclusions
- Learn how characters deal with conflict, solve problems, and relate to real-life situations
- Compare and contrast the languages, arts, and customs of different cultures
- Observe good speaking skills
- Analyze the ways the mind, body, and voice are used to communicate character, setting, and emotions

The power and the magic of storytelling connect the past with the present and the future. Storytelling creates community; it is a means for passing on the values and morals of cultures. And storytelling is a vital educational tool for helping all students succeed.

***Sue Black** combines her passion for storytelling with her delight in teaching students and their teachers to tell stories. In school residencies, she takes students from page to stage. In her workshops for educators, Sue details storytelling and its connection to the Illinois Learning Standards, Bloom's Taxonomy, and the writing process. www.storytelling.org/Black*

Storytelling in Science and Math

by Barbara Lipke

Storytelling can be used in teaching subject matter all across the curriculum, including science and math. Stories carry information which students will remember far better than they would facts on a worksheet or in a lecture. The scientific method itself, nature studies, biographies of scientists and mathematicians, and mathematical concepts may all be successfully addressed through stories.

The basic philosophy of science is the scientific method, in which hypotheses are formed and then tested with experiments, validating or disproving them. You might illustrate the scientific method – and explore the properties of a gooey material – using *Bartholomew and the Oobleck* by Dr. Seuss (NY: Random House, 1949). After telling the story, ask the students what else they want to know about oobleck. List, categorize, and prioritize their questions, and have them design experiments to answer the questions.

Follow the steps below to investigate the scientific method in a variety of ways.

1. Tell a story. Almost any story. Ask your students what else they want to know about that story.
2. Write all of their questions on the board.
3. Categorize the questions. Discuss the categories. (Some questions may fit into more than one.)
4. Determine which category is most important and explore it first. Arrange the questions in order of priority.
5. Choose a question, and ask the students what experiments they could use to find the answer to it. Be sure to record reasons for their experiments. These are hypotheses.
6. Discuss the projected experiments. Decide which one will be most useful in answering your question. Emphasize the importance of keeping accurate records of actions and observations.

7. Impress on students the importance of replicating their experiments and be sure they understand why this is necessary. If they carry out the experiments, ask a different group of students to try to reproduce them.

Tell stories about nature, scientists, and scientific discoveries. How and why stories from many cultures illustrate early explanations of the world. Tell some of these. Then, with your students, brainstorm a list of natural phenomena (for example: lightning, rainbows, insect metamorphosis, ripening of fruit). Have students create and tell their own myths. Then have them research the scientific explanation for the occurrences.

Good scientists do experiment after experiment, testing hypotheses. They may have to defend their ideas in the face of criticism; it may be years before new ideas are accepted. For example, Robert Koch performed 605 unsuccessful experiments in his search for a chemical compound to treat syphilis. Louis Pasteur's theory that microbes cause illness was at first ridiculed. Sometimes scientists face ethical problems. Crick and Watson, who won the Nobel prize for their efforts, gave no credit to Rosalind Franklin whose work led to their model for DNA. Tell the stories of issues scientists face. Have your students debate these problems or hold a mock trial to investigate the topics.

Math curricula, too, can benefit from the introduction of stories. Mathematical concepts and arithmetic are everywhere! Use well-known fairytales, picture books, or create your own tales. Tell your students a story and ask them to find the math applications in it. With "Rapunzel," for example, they may ask how high the tower was, how long Rapunzel's hair was (braided or loose), how strong her hair had to be (how many pounds it could support), how much the old crone weighed, and so on. Have students work in pairs on problems based on their own questions. Have them exchange problems with others and work on solutions. The fact that students have created their own problems motivates their work.

Some stories have a specific mathematical application. These include counting rhymes and stories of halving and doubling, large and small numbers, fractions, geometry, and exponents.

One Grain of Rice by Demi (NY: Scholastic Press, 1997) relates the story of a peasant girl who asks to be rewarded with a single grain of rice, to be doubled every day for a month. Soon the raja is nearly bankrupt! Create and tell your own stories to motivate students' exploration of estimation, measurement, exponents, etc. Or have students create "word problems," stories that contain math ideas.

Venn diagrams are important mathematical constructs which use overlapping circles to show the relationship between sets. The overlapping areas represent shared information. To illustrate this, ask students for a well-known story (for example, "Aladdin"). Have them list the story elements on strips of paper. Then tell them a different version of the story and have them list the details. Students arrange the strips so that the elements common to both versions are in the middle, with others to the outside. When they circle each version's strips, they create a Venn diagram.

Involve the students in the drama of history: tell stories of mathematical discoveries or the lives and times of mathematicians. Galileo's mathematical proof that the earth traveled around the sun put his life in jeopardy with the Inquisition. *Galileo's Daughter* by Dava Sobel is a good source of information. (NY: Walker & Co., 1999.)

Science and math are exciting. They are the stuff of curiosity, and we were all born with large doses of curiosity! Scientists and mathematicians don't know all the answers. They are curious folks looking for answers. And where do you and they find the questions to ask? In the world around us, including the world of story.

*Barbara Lipke, Storyteller/Educational Consultant, taught elementary school for twenty-four years in Brookline, MA. Now she tells, coaches, and teaches students and teachers about the power of storytelling. This article was excerpted and adapted from her book, **Figures, Facts and Fables: Telling Tales in Science and Math**, Portsmouth, NH: Heinemann, 1996, and used by permission. Barbara can be reached at bliptales@earthlink.net.*

The Waldorf Schools Philosophy

by Janaka Stagnaro

"The pass was blocked by a wall of snow. Ten days now in the harsh mountains of the Alps. Already, many of his men have perished from the cold winds and snow in this land so different from the warm sun of Carthage."

The teacher stops and looks out over the faces of his sixth grade class like a general, his posture erect, his hands on his hips.

"'Men,' Hannibal said to the huddled troops, 'we could turn back now and go home to our wives and feel the warmth of the sun. But we would come back as losers, as those who turned away from hardship. And most likely we would see Roman galleys come into our bay and destroy our city . . . Yes, many will die in this foreign land, but your names will live as men who died with giants.'" The teacher lifts his arm as if beckoning forward. "And with this, the elephants trumpeted and the men cheered."

The teacher lowers his arm. In a quiet voice he says, "And tomorrow we'll hear what happened."

****

"Children, today we will be studying about Hannibal of Carthage, who in the Second Punic War fought Rome. In 218 B.C., Hannibal commanded a force of 50,000 men and forty elephants and marched for fifteen days over the Alps. Take out your textbooks and turn to page 85 . . . "

****

These two scenarios both teach the history of Hannibal. The first is an example of what one would find in a Waldorf school. The second is what one may experience in many other classrooms. In the first, children are riveted to their seats, staring at the teacher with rapt attention. They have been transported back in time, out of their seats, and into the Alps, seeing themselves freezing in the snow or encouraging their men to push forward.

In the second case, children are listening to facts on which they will be tested. Many will open their books with sighs. Some will be keen to read, but many will disengage as they hear about Hannibal's first victories at Ticinus and Trebia; Hannibal has nothing to do with them personally. He is only a dead factoid, perhaps a point on a test or in a game of *Trebia* Pursuit (pun intended).

The 800-plus Waldorf schools around the world teach to the whole child for her physical, emotional, mental, and spiritual needs. Whether it is in the kindergarten or in the elementary levels, this multi-faceted teaching pivots around storytelling.

In kindergarten, the children are told the same story numerous times over a whole week or more. The story is told with the same words and nuances; in the early years children thrive on repetition and rhythm. If the teacher strays from the text, the children will correct the error. Children reenact the story through free play. The rich language of the tale permeates their consciousness, like rain filtering through fertile soil. As one Waldorf teacher put it, "Stories in kindergarten are used to calm upset children, to tickle imaginations into healthy play, to help develop empathy and reverence for others, to nourish, guide, and advise in a non-direct manner, and to support the incarnation of the soul through fairy tales."

In the elementary grades, "learning blocks" may last two to six weeks. These units are taught in a two-hour morning session called Main Lesson; a fifteen-minute story is usually told at the end. After intensely focusing on the main lesson, the child is allowed to breathe out and to be empty while absorbing the story. The children take the story images home, and because Waldorf families generally agree that no media viewing will occur during the school week, they take the images into sleep, allowing the unconscious mind to work with the story. The next morning the children recapitulate the story. This is done in an artistic manner, through drawing, pantomiming, writing, sculpting, and more.

Rudolf Steiner, the founder of Waldorf education in 1919, suggested that stories correspond to the developmental needs of each grade. He did not want stories told for entertainment's sake. Story time is a sacred time. Often the lights go down, a candle is lit, a poem is recited or a song is sung, and perhaps an instrument like a lyre or flute is played. The children are nourished with characters and their worlds.

Stories can create a rich tapestry of language, provide character-building experiences, and bring to life pictures illustrating many subjects of the curriculum. Perhaps the most important element of storytelling in the Waldorf system is that the teacher stands completely exposed before the children. The teacher's own biography reveals itself unconsciously while he tells the tale; through body language, tone, memory, language use, and many other nuances.

Waldorf education is about growing up a well-rounded, free, questioning human being. Children learn best not from machines or media, but by being with people, listening to their stories, and watching how they fail and succeed. From the dreaminess of European fairy tales, to the Indian tale of Rama rescuing Sita, to exploring the northwest wilderness with Lewis and Clark, each story told is an initiation into the mysteries of life and a means of creating lifetime explorers.

*Janaka Stagnaro is the author of **Silent Ripples: Parables for the Soul** and **Footprints Along the Shore of an Incoming Tide**. A Waldorf teacher, poet, artist, storyteller, and mentor, he lives in Monterey, California. You can see his work at www.janakastagnaro.com.*

Storytelling as a Therapeutic Tool

by Judith Margerum

Most storytelling can be therapeutic. Stories that are told in schools and libraries may be the same stories told to a child in therapy. The picture books *The Little Engine That Could*[1] and *Rainbow Fish,*[2] Cinderella stories, and Andersen's "The Ugly Duckling" all have therapeutic messages about the strength, beauty, and courage inside us all.

Children learn differently from adults. Talking about problems is an adult behavior. Children learn through play, by pretending and imagining. They often resolve grief and life struggles through play. They may recreate a scenario over and over until they have mastered it. They may want a story read or told multiple times until they have internalized it.

Storytelling takes listeners to a different level of awareness. Their eyes are wide, their mouths are slightly open, and they are very focused. When children are in this trancelike state their minds are open. It is the perfect time to introduce ideas that might not be accepted if given more directly. Ideas slip into the unconscious without the child even knowing they have done so.

Storytelling in Therapy

The purpose of therapeutic storytelling is healing and growth. Stories told in therapy grow out of the therapist's relationship with the child. They spring from the child's strengths, weaknesses, and struggles. Real life stories, personal stories, fairy tales, or stories specifically created with or for the child can be equally effective. In telling a story the therapist is planting a seed. It is the therapist's job to choose which seeds to plant. The seeds of hope and possibility are present in many stories; they can be vital to those who struggle with life.

When problems are addressed directly, defenses may go up. Even constructive criticism is often viewed as an attack by a vulnerable child. Telling a story about a problem that someone else is experiencing takes the focus off the child. The child remains open to the character's struggles, journey, and attempted resolutions, because this is a character in a story, not the child herself.

The classic Italian fantasy "Pinocchio" addresses telling lies in an imaginative and childlike way, while Aesop's "The Boy Who Cried Wolf" is a classic cautionary tale. *There's a Monster Under My Bed*[3] takes a humorous look at childhood fears. The most significant fear, that of losing a parent, is made accessible through Grimm's "Hansel and Gretel," Disney's "Bambi," and the many versions of Cinderella.

In *The Little Engine that Could*, the repetition of the phrase "I think I can, I think I can," reinforces a child's internal strength. My own son encouraged himself by repeating this phrase while on a strenuous backpacking trip! *Bunny Trouble*[4] is a story of how a bunny who is different can find a way to fit in and still maintain his special gifts. Disney's classic "Dumbo" and *Leo the Lop*[5] also deal with being different.

Hearing stories can help children feel love, guilt, fear, empathy, or sadness without becoming lost in these emotions. Stories can be cathartic or help children re-interpret their life. They can inspire children's courage to be themselves or to become unstuck from their problems. "Bambi" and "Hansel and Gretel" deal with grief and loss. *The Velveteen Rabbit*[6] deals with abandonment, change, and growing up.

Sometimes the most meaningful story is one created by the therapist with the child. Creating a story with a child allows him to have some control over what the hero is like, what happens to him on his journey, and the outcome of the story. Children often feel little control over their lives; this allows them to experience a sense of control. If the story hits home, the child feels truly understood.

Classrooms and Recreational Groups

Outside of traditional therapy, storytelling in classrooms or recreational groups can provide models for character development and solutions to everyday problems. A teacher, volunteer, or storyteller who knows his audience can choose tales which address issues such as bullying, loss, fear of failure and embarrassment, and feeling left out. However, if a student is experiencing severe distress, becomes physically aggressive, or exhibits signs of depression, psychologically trained personnel should be notified.

Bobby and Sherry Norfolk discuss the use of storytelling in character development in their book *The Moral of the Story*[7]. Their "The Billy Goats Gruff" rap deals with bullying. The Hasidic story "Feathers"[8] is ideal for the middle school issue of gossiping; it compares the spread of gossip to the feathers from a pillow which are scattered by the wind. "The Blind Men and the Elephant" is a folktale from China and India in which each man understands only part of the truth.

Storytelling in these settings may provide alternate ways to view hardship and weakness, find solutions to conflict and struggle, and encourage hope – which boosts the resilience of all children. Most of all, storytelling should foster the appreciation of the strength, beauty, and courage inside us all.

Notes

1. Watty Piper, et al. *The Little Engine That Could*. NY: Platt and Munk, 1976.
2. Marcus Pfister. *Rainbow Fish*. NY: North-South Books, 1992.
3. James Howe. *There's a Monster Under My Bed*. NY: Aladdin Paperbacks, 1986.
4. Hans Wilhelm. *Bunny Trouble*. NY: Scholastic Inc., 1985.
5. Stephen Cosgrove and Robin James. *Leo the Lop*. Danbury: Grolier, 1979.
6. Margery Williams. *The Velveteen Rabbit*, NY: Bantam, Doubleday, Dell, 1991.
7. Bobby and Sherry Norfolk. *The Moral of the Story: Folktales for Character Development*. AR: August House, 1999.
8. Heather Forest. *Wisdom Tales From Around the World*. AR: August House, 1996

Judith Margerum has been a psychologist for over twenty years, working with families and children She has performed and led workshops on the use of storytelling in therapy in various settings throughout Michigan. Judith is a single mother of two teenage boys who also love stories. *margerumj@sbcglobal.net*

A Spoonful of Story Helps the Medicine Go Down

by Kimberley King

I first learned how a spoonful of story can sweeten an unpleasant task when I was a teenaged babysitter. The parents had hinted that their toddler might resist going to bed. (Translation: Expect a Battle Royal at bedtime.) Sure enough, when bedtime was announced, the child opened his mouth to scream. But before he could let out a sound, I inserted, "Your Mommy and Daddy are not going to believe how grown up you were." The child looked startled, but interested. "When I tell them that you got ready for bed *all by yourself* and didn't make any noise at all, they are going to think that some other boy has come to live here! They are going to say, 'Are you *sure*? Not *any* noise?' They will be so proud!"

Dear Reader, it worked. That child put on his pajamas, brushed his teeth, listened to his story, and went to bed without a peep.

Years later my young son had to go to the hospital during a bout of croup. The first time it happened it took three adults to hold him down. The second time I said, "Of course, you are so much more grown up now that you will be Very Brave. The people at the hospital are not going to believe you are the same guy who was here last week. When they see you can even *put the mask on yourself* they are going to be so amazed. 'Wow! He's so grown up!' they're going to think." They did, too.

For cleaning up, I invented "Fastman and his Brother," the fastest toy-picker-uppers in town! In the state! In the country! In the *entire world*!" I narrated Fastman's progress as if I were the announcer at a basketball game. "And Fastman aims for the box with the bears, he shoots, he misses, he moves in . . . and he *scores*!"

A favorite morning story went like this: "This morning . . . *reeeally* early . . . before I was even awake . . . I heard a NOISE. (whimper like small child waking up) and *some*thing went

THUMP. Pad pad pad pad pad. And then *something crrreeeeped* into my bed . . . ." (Child shouts, "It was me!")

They never tired of this one. Nor did they tire of hearing stories about how they were born, or of things they did: funny, bad, good, real, or imaginary. These stories rooted them in the larger world: they were heroes of their own narrative.

My sons also loved hearing about their parents when they were little, especially "Bad Mommy" or "Bad Daddy" stories. They liked the story of how their Dad and his brother shot the garage full of BBs – and spent a good part of the summer digging them out and re-painting the garage – or about the time I painted my sister with peanut butter. They found great comfort in knowing that in pre-historic times their parents were children who got into trouble, too.

As the kids got older, I created stories which mirrored their lives in more complicated ways. My younger son didn't like kindergarten. At home, I began to tell him stories about a mouse. The mouse went to kindergarten every day, against the rules, smuggled in inside a small boy's pocket. Once there, the mouse was quite naughty – stealing bites of the children's snacks, eating crayons, getting into the finger paint, squeaking when the children were supposed to be quiet. That mouse got to do all the things a small boy would have *liked* to do in the classroom, but couldn't. He became a kind of comfort toy – because an invisible, imaginary mouse can go anywhere, even to school. Although my son still didn't like kindergarten, the mouse stories helped him to feel comforted and understood.

In first grade, my son got in trouble for fighting. A story about a dragon grew from this. The dragon was angry, bad-tempered, and fierce. It sank its claws into a boy's back and whispered in his ear, "Hit him! Bite him! Kick him!" It never let up. It was always nearby – waiting. I asked my son to help with the story. What do you do with a dragon who is hungry and mean and who will never leave you alone? He thought we should feed it, "because maybe if it wasn't hungry all the time it wouldn't be so mean." "What do dragons eat?" "Pizza!"

The boy in the story lured the dragon with pepperoni pizza. Once the dragon had eaten several pieces he was in a much better humor. As dragon and boy became friends they began to play together instead of fighting with other people. My son was learning that you can't necessarily get rid of anger, but you can learn to live with it. The fighting ended soon after.

A little imagination works miracles. A soupçon of story makes ordinary tasks more fun and eases difficult situations. Stories about family give children a sense of security and belonging. Stories about their lives help them to understand that what they do is important, and that they have the power to direct their own experience. Working in the world of metaphor provides a safe way for young children to process feelings that they can't tackle directly. Stories like these put imagination into action, create connections, and sweeten the soul.

Kimberley King is a storyteller in Bend, Oregon. She was co-founder of Arts of Passage, an inter-disciplinary arts program for at-risk youth. She is a mother, musician writer, and closet poet. She still has a day job. yelrebmik@earthlink.net

The following is a small, annotated selection of the many story collections and books of advice on telling to children. Some are out of print but may be available in libraries. Please note, too, the publications cited throughout this book – they are not duplicated here. Space also prevents us from listing picture books. Audio recordings and videos can be found at tellers' websites or from the publishers cited below. Entries without descriptions are annotated in *A Beginner's Guide to Storytelling* edited by Katy Rydell. An unabridged and periodically updated version of this bookshelf is available at the NSN website, www.storynet.org. Enjoy!

Storytelling Theory and Practice

Bauer, Caroline Feller. *Caroline Feller Bauer's New Handbook for Storytellers: with Stories, Poems, Magic, and More*. Chicago: American Library Association, 1995.

Collins, Rives and Pamela J. Cooper. *The Power of Story: Teaching Through Storytelling*. 2nd edition. Needham Heights, MA: Allyn and Bacon, 1997.

Davis, Donald. *Telling Your Own Stories: For Family and Classroom Storytelling, Public Speaking, and Personal Journaling*. Little Rock, AR: August House, 1993.

Dailey, Sheila, ed. *Tales as Tools: the Power of Story in the Classroom*. Jonesborough, TN: National Storytelling Press, 1994. Storytelling in reading, writing, history, science, math, language development, multicultural education, social and environmental education, and the creation of classroom communities. Also: *Putting the World in a Nutshell: The Art of the Formula Tale*.

de Vos, Gail. *Storytelling for Young Adults: A Guide to Tales for Teens*. Westport, CT: Libraries Unlimited, 2003. Telling stories to adolescents, ages 13 to 18. Why tell to teens, selecting stories, what to expect from the audience, story lists, and "teen-tested" ready-to-tell stories.

Greene, Ellin. *Storytelling Art & Technique*. Westport, CT: Libraries Unlimited, 1996. 3rd edition. Textbook on the value of storytelling, story selection, preparation, presentation to various age groups, and children with special needs. Focus on telling in libraries.

MacDonald, Margaret Read. *The Parent's Guide to Storytelling: How to Make Up New Stories and Retell Old Favorites*. Little Rock, AR: August House, 2001. Also: *Storyteller's Start-Up Book: Finding, Learning, Performing, and Using Folktales*.

Moore, Robin. *Creating a Family Storytelling Tradition: Awakening the Hidden Storyteller*. Little Rock, AR: August House, 1999. Suggestions for telling stories at home with the family using "voyages" into the imagination to locate, select, and prepare story sources.

Rydell, Katy, ed. *A Beginner's Guide to Storytelling*. Jonesborough, TN: National Storytelling Press, 2003. Compact guide from the National Storytelling Network, first in this series. Choosing and developing stories, program planning, stage fright, voice care, and more.

Sima, Judy and Kevin Cordi. *Raising Voices: Youth Storytelling Groups and Troupes*. Westport, CT: Libraries Unlimited, 2002. Step-by-step guide for student storytelling clubs. Reproducible activities, learning stories, coaching and fundraising.

Zeitlin, Steven J., Amy J. Kotkin, and Holly Cutting Baker. *A Celebration of American Family Folklore: Tales and Traditions from the Smithsonian Collection*. NY: Pantheon Books, 1982. More than 2,000 family interviews 1974 to 1977. How Americans interpret their history. Interviewing guide; sample questionnaire for collecting family lore.

Storytelling Collections

Brody, Ed, ed., et al. *Spinning Tales Weaving Hope: Stories, Storytelling and Activities for Peace, Justice, & the Environment*. Philadelphia: New Society Publisher, 2002. Twenty-nine multicultural stories with follow-ups for writing, music, drama, and crafts. Promoting self-esteem, compassion, conflict resolution, and sensitivity to all living things.

Cabral, Len and Mia Manduca. *Len Cabral's Storytelling Book*. NY: Neal-Schumann, 1997. Twenty-three familiar and not-so familiar stories from Africa and other traditions. Directions for telling stories and activities to integrate them into the curriculum.

Caduto, Michael J. *Earth Tales from Around the World*. Golden, CO: Fulcrum, 1997. Organized into ten themes such as Earth, Water, Sky, Plants, Fire, and Wisdom. Stories from every continent. Suggestions for lessons and further exploration.

Caduto, Michael J. and Joseph Bruchac. *Keepers of the Earth: Native American Stories and Environmental Activities for Children*. Golden, CO: Fulcrum, 1988.

Carle, Eric. *Treasury of Classic Stories for Children*. NY: Orchard Books, 1996. Twenty-two familiar and not so familiar tales by Aesop, the Grimm brothers, and Hans Christian Andersen, collected and illustrated by a Caldecott-winning illustrator.

Climo, Shirley. *A Treasury of Princesses: Princess Tales from Around the World*. NY: HarperCollins, 1996. Retellings of seldom-heard princess tales. A discussion of princess lore precedes each selection. Also: *A Treasury of Mermaids: Mermaid Tales from Around the World*.

Cohn, Amy L. *From Sea to Shining Sea: A Treasury of American Folklore and Songs*. NY: Scholastic, 1993. Includes creation stories, scary stories, tall tales, Revolutionary War, slavery, pioneers, immigrants, and baseball.

Cole, Joanna. ***Best-Loved Folktales of the World***. Garden City, NY: Doubleday, 1982.

Courlander, Harold and George Herzog. ***The Cow-Tail Switch and Other West African Stories***. NY: Henry Holt, 1986.

DeSpain, Pleasant. ***Sweet Land of Story: Thirty-Six American Tales to Tell***. Little Rock, AR: August House, 2000. Stories spanning the nation, ranging from practical and wise to silly and scary; including Civil War heroes, Native American traditions, and Old West tales. Also: ***Eleven Nature Tales; The Emerald Lizard; The Books of Nine Lives; Thirty-Three Multicultural Tales to Tell***.

Fujita, Hiroko. Adapted and edited by Fran Stalling. ***Stories to Play With: Kids' Tales Told with Puppets, Paper, Toys, and Imagination***. Little Rock, AR: August House, 1999. Short, easy-to-tell tales for young children using drawing, participation, and common materials. Some well-known stories, some stories from Japan. Easy-to-follow diagrams.

Hamilton, Virginia. ***The People Could Fly: American Black Folktales***. NY: Knopf, 1985. Twenty-four tales from the African American tradition: Bruh Rabbit, slave tales of freedom, tales of the supernatural. Told with a hint of dialect. Source notes. Also: ***Her Stories: African American Folktales, Fair Tales, and True Tales***.

Haven, Kendall. ***Voices of the American Civil War: Stories of Men, Women, and Children Who Lived Through the War Between the States***. Westport, CT: Libraries Unlimited, 2002. Twenty-seven historically accurate accounts of men, women, and children from the North and South during the Civil War. Follow-up questions, projects, activities, and discussion points. Also: ***Voices of the American Revolution***.

Haviland, Virginia. ***Favorite Fairy Tales Told in Norway***. NY: Beech Tree Books, 1995. Seven easy-to-read stories adaptable for telling. Part of the ***Favorite Fairy Tales***

Told In series. Other books in the series: France, England, Germany, India, Ireland, Sweden, Poland, Russia, Spain, Czechoslovakia, Scotland, Denmark, Japan, Greece, and Italy.

Holbrook, Belinda. *String Stories: A Creative, Hands-On Approach for Engaging Children in Literature*. Worthington, OH: Linworth Publishing, 2002. Nineteen string stories with step-by-step directions from the easiest to the most complex.

Holt, David and Bill Mooney, eds. *Ready-To-Tell Tales: Sure-Fire Stories from America's Favorite Storytellers*. Little Rock, AR: August House, 1994.

Jacobs, Joseph. *English Fairy Tales*. NY: Dover Dell, 1967.

Jaffe, Nina and Steve Zeitlin. *The Cow of No Color: Riddle Stories and Justice Tales from Around the World*. NY: Henry Holt, 1998. Stories from Asia, Africa, Europe, and North America give readers the opportunity to play judge and jury by answering the question at the end of each tale. Also: *While Standing on One Foot: Puzzle Stories and Wisdom Tales from the Jewish Tradition*.

Justice, Jennifer, ed. *The Ghost & I: Scary Stories for Participatory Telling*. Cambridge, MA: Yellow Moon Press, 1992.

Lewis, Shari. *One-Minute Bedtime Stories*. Garden City, NY: Doubleday, 1982. Twenty compact, easy-to-tell versions of familiar and not so familiar tales, including: Rumpelstiltskin, Paul Bunyan, the Golden Goose, Lion and the Mouse, and Sorcerer's Apprentice.

Livo, Norma J. *Story Medicine: Multicultural Tales of Healing and Transformation*. Westport, CT: Libraries Unlimited, 2001. Forty tales from around the world chosen to promote wellness and happiness. Includes reading guidance, reflection, and discussion starters for each story. Also: *Bringing Out Their Best: Values Education and Character Development through Traditional Tales*.

Lobel, Arnold. *Fables*. NY: Harper Trophy, 1983. Twenty original fables about an array of animal characters from crocodile to ostrich.

Loya, Olga. *Momentos Magicos, Magic Moments: Tales from Latin America Told in English and Spanish*. Little Rock, AR: August House, 1997. Fifteen stories. Scary stories, tricksters, strong women, and myths from Mexico, Guatemala, Nicaragua, Puerto Rico, Cuba, Colombia, and the Mayan, Chol, and Aztec peoples.

MacDonald, Margaret Read. *Twenty Tellable Tales: Audience Participation Folktales for the Beginning Storyteller*. NY: H. W. Wilson, 1986.

Marsh, Valerie. *Storyteller's Sampler*. Fort Atkinson, WI: Alleyside Press (available through Highsmith Press), 1996. Four stories for each of five story types – paper cutting, mystery fold, sign language, story puzzles, and storyknifing. Easy-to-follow patterns. Great for young audiences and the "artistically challenged." Also: *Beyond Words: Great Stories for Hand and Voice*.

Martin, Rafe. *Mysterious Tales of Japan*. NY: Putnam, 1996. Ten evocative stories retold by one of America's best-known author/storytellers. Also: *The Hungry Tigress: Buddhist Tales and Legends*.

Mead, Erica Helm. *The Moon in the Well: Wisdom Tales to Transform Your Life, Family, and Community*. Chicago: Open Court Publishing, 2001. Sixty-five folktales with healing applications drawn from the author's counseling experience. Theme index suggesting more stories about similar issues.

Miller, Theresa. *Joining In: An Anthology of Audience Participation Stories & How to Tell Them*. Cambridge, MA: Yellow Moon Press, 1988.

Orgel, Doris. *The Lion and the Mouse and Other Aesop Fables*. NY: DK Publishers, 2001. Twelve familiar Aesop fables. Information on the life and times of Aesop.

Osborne, Mary Pope and Troy Howell. ***Favorite Medieval Tales***. NY: Scholastic, 1998. Nine illustrated retellings of well-known tales from the European Middle Ages including Beowulf, Robin Hood, and Finn MacCoul. Also: ***Mermaid Tales from Around the World***.

Pellowski, Anne. ***The Story Vine; a Source Book of Unusual and Easy-to-Tell Stories from Around the World***. NY: Macmillan, 1984. Stories using string, nesting dolls, African thumb piano, riddles, finger games, drawing, and sand painting. Includes string stories The Mosquito and The Yam Farmer. Also: ***The Family Storytelling Handbook: How To Use Stories, Anecdotes, Rhymes, Handkerchiefs, Paper, and Other Objects to Enrich Family Traditions***.

San Souci, Robert D. ***Cut From the Same Cloth: American Women of Myth, Legend, and Tall Tale***. NY: Philomel Books, 1993. Fifteen tales of strong-willed women from Anglo-American, African American, Spanish American, and Native American traditions. Also: ***Short & Shivery: Thirty Chilling Tales; More Short and Shivery; Still More Short and Shivery; Even More Short and Shivery***.

Shannon, George. ***Stories to Solve: Folktales from Around the World***. NY: Greenwillow Books, 1985. Fifteen brief folktales are presented in which there is a mystery, problem, or riddle to solve before the solution is given. These stories make good "fillers." Also: ***More Stories to Solve; Still More Stories to Solve; True Lies***.

Sherman, Josepha. ***Trickster Tales: Forty Folk Stories from Around the World***. Little Rock, AR: August House, 1996. Forty stories from every continent and many cultures including ancient Babylonia, China, India, Eastern Europe, Morocco and others. Notes on origins and motifs. Also: ***Once Upon a Galaxy; Rachel the Clever and Other Jewish Folktales.***

Singer, Isaac Bashevis. ***Stories for Children***. NY: Farrar, Straus and Giroux, 1984. Thirty-six stories from life, legend, and fantasy by Nobel Prize winning Yiddish writer. Includes stories of Chelm, a city of fools; stories from the Polish shtetl (Jewish village); and Bible stories. Also: ***Zlateh the Goat and Other Stories***.

Spagnoli, Cathy. ***Terrific Trickster Tales from Asia***. Fort Atkinson, WI: Alleyside Press (available through Highsmith Press), 2001. Twenty-six easy-to-tell, authentic tales from seventeen nations along with cultural background, storytelling techniques, and learning activities. Also: ***A Treasury of Asian Stories and Activities: A Guide for Schools and Libraries***.

Weaver, Mary C., ed. ***Many Voices: True Tales From America's Past***. Jonesborough, TN: National Storytelling Press, 1995. Thirty-six historical tales from 1643 to 1989, about actual or fictional characters. Stories include: Abraham Lincoln, Sacagawea, Scott Joplin, Sitting Bull, Rosie the Riveter, others. Companion volume with worksheets and activities: ***Many Voices Teacher's Guide***.

World Folklore Series. Westport, CT: Libraries Unlimited.

Yep, Laurence. ***The Rainbow People***. NY: Harper Trophy, 1992. Twenty Chinese and Chinese-American stories from Kwangtung Province. Tricksters, Fools, Virtues and Vices, In Chinese America, and Love.

Yolen, Jane. ***Not One Damsel in Distress: World Folktales from Strong Girls***. San Diego, CA: Silver Whistle Books, 2000. Thirteen tales of clever, heroic, and ingenious young women from Europe, Asia, the Americas, and Africa. Also: ***Mightier than the Sword: World Folktales for Strong Boys; Favorite Folktales from Around the World***.

Young, Richard and Judy Dockery Young. ***Race with Buffalo: and Other Native American Stories for Young Readers***. Little Rock, AR: August House, 1994. Thirty-one easy-to-tell Native American stories about how and why, ancient times, young heroes, tricksters, and the spirit world from Cherokee, Choctaw, Seneca, Iroquois, and other traditions. Also: ***Stories from the Days of Christopher***

Columbus; African American Folktales for Young Readers; Favorite Scary Stories of American Children.

Publishers and Distributors – Books and Recordings

August House. P.O. Box 3223, Little Rock, AR 72203-3223. 800-284-8784. www.augusthouse.com

Fulcrum Publishing. 350 Indiana Street, Suite 350, Golden, CO 80401-5093. 800-992-2908. www.fulcrum-resources.com

A Gentle Wind: Songs and Stories for Children. P. O. Box 3103, Albany, NY 12203. 888-386-7664. www.gentlewind.com

Highsmith Press. W5527 State Road106, P.O. Box 800, Fort Atkinson, WI 53538. 800-558-2110. www.hpress.highsmith.com

Libraries Unlimited. 80 Post Road East, P.O. Box 5007, Westport, CT 06881-5007. 800-225-5800. www.lu.com

National Storytelling Press. 132 Boone Street, Jonesborough, TN 37659. 800-525-4514. www.storynet.org

Shen's Books. 40951 Fremont Blvd., Fremont, CA 94538. 800-456-6660. www.shens.com

Shoe String Press. 2 Linsley Street, North Haven, CT 06473-2517. 203-239-2702. SSPBooks@aol.com

Yellow Moon Press. P.O. Box 1316, Cambridge, MA 02238. 617-776-2230. www.yellowmoon.com

Websites of Interest
compiled by Karen Chace

Absolutely Whootie: Stories to Grow By
Multicultural folktales searchable by continent and country, free writing assignments, and play scripts. It also offers stories categorized by themes to foster positive behavior and reinforcement. http://storiestogrowby.com

Australian Storytelling
Site of the Australian Storytelling Guild with articles, interviews, a newsletter, a calendar of events, and links to related resources on the Internet. www.australianstorytelling.org.au

The Baldwin Project
Nursery rhymes, fables, folktales, myths, legends and hero stories, literary fairy tales, bible stories, nature stories, biography, history, fiction, poetry, storytelling, games, and craft activities. The works of such luminaries as Padraic Colum, Howard Pyle, Andrew Lang, and James Baldwin at your fingertips. www.mainlesson.com/main/displayarticle. php?article=christmas

The Children's Literature Web Guide
Lots of storytelling information, teaching tools, book lists and links. www.ucalgary.ca/~dkbrown

Eldrbarry's Storytelling Page
A never-ending wealth of resources and links for the beginner to the advanced storyteller. www.eldrbarry.net

Enoch Pratt Libraries
Listen to some of our most beloved storytellers share their tales in streaming video. A delight for children and adults! www.epfl.net/kids/estories/ESTORIES_archive_list.cfm

How to Tell Stories to Children
The electronic text of Sara Cone Bryant's book, offered through the University of Virginia Library website. The book, published in 1915, still offers wonderful advice for beginning tellers. Stories are categorized by age groups up

to fifth grade. http://etext.lib.virginia.edu/toc/modeng/public/BryTell.html

Once Upon A Time

Enjoy some of the old classics here. Short, easy to tell tales. http://xrules.com/library/fairytales/index.html

Storynet.org

The official site for the National Storytelling Network. Gives advice on becoming a storyteller and offers storytelling news, links, grant and award information; a directory of tellers; lists of books, magazines and tapes, local guilds and regional organizations; as well as full information on the National Storytelling Festival in Jonesborough TN and the annual National Storytelling Conference. www.storynet.org

Storyteller.net

A great site; includes articles, events calendar, interviews, and you can even hear tellers tell! www.storyteller.net

Storytelling Arts of Indiana

Teaching guides, games, activities, and resources from such quality tellers as Heather Forest, Doug Lipman, Rex Ellis, Doug Elliott, Janice Harrington, and Ed Stivender. www.storytellingarts.org/TeachersGuide.html

Tales of Wonder

A collection of stories from around the world: across the African plains, into the mysterious East, then over to the Emerald Isles. www.darsie.net/talesofwonder

Teaching with Folklore Index

An entry point for teachers to use folklore Internet resources with their class. Geared mainly to elementary grades one to six. Activities, lesson plans, stories, and extensions are all here. www.qesn.meq.gouv.qc.ca/folklore/index.htm

Tell Me A Story

Unique stories from around the world, adapted by Amy Friedman and Jillian Gilliland. www.uexpress.com/tellmeastory

Turner Learning Network

An Educator's Guide to Storytelling; tips on teaching storytelling, national standards, assessments and cross-curricular approaches. A good resource for integrated storytelling into curriculum.www.turnerlearning.com/turnersouth/storytelling/index.html

Index